W9-CTR-469

LEADING FROM THE MAZE

To Vicki,

LEADING
FROM THE
MAZE

A Personal Pathway to Leadership

In celebration of the "teacher within".

JEFFREY PATNAUDE

Jeff Patnaude

TEN SPEED PRESS
BERKELEY, CALIFORNIA

Copyright © 1996 by Jeffrey Patnaude.
Foreword © 1996 by John Archer.

All rights reserved. No part of this book
may be reproduced in any form, except
brief excerpts for the purpose of review,
without written permission of the
publisher.

Ten Speed Press
P.O. Box 7123
Berkeley, California 94707

Distributed in Australia by E. J. Dwyer
Pty. Ltd., in Canada by Publishers Group
West, in New Zealand by Tandem Press,
in South Africa by Real Books, and in
the United Kingdom and Europe by
Airlift Books.

Cover design by Cale Burr
Interior design by Sarah Levin
Illustrations by Diana Reiss

LIBRARY OF CONGRESS CATALOGING-
IN-PUBLICATION DATA

Patnaude, Jeff.
    Leading from the Maze /
Jeffrey Patnaude
        p.   cm.
    ISBN 0-89815-745-5
        1. Leadership.
        2. Executive ability.
        3. Success in business
        4. Self-reliance.
        5. Introspection. I. Title.
    HD57.7.P367 1996   95-45433
    658.4'09—dc20   CIP

First printing, 1996
Printed in the United States of America

1 2 3 4 5 6 7 8 9 10 — 00 99 98 97 96

To my two beautiful daughters,
Julie and Laura.

Acknowledgments

One of the most important components of my life has been the mentors who have walked the maze ahead of me and provoked my participation. This book would not be a reality without the support of two people: Dr. John Archer, friend, priest, professor, and creative mind who helped shape this work, and Jesse Phillips, friend and guide who believed in and supported this project long before I understood its implications.

Contents

FOREWORD:

On Jeffrey Patnaude and the EAGLES Seminars

THREE YEARS AGO, on a sunny March morning, I paid a call on a friend. I had sought him out to help me uncover new possibilities in my life, having decided to leave a profession that had fed and sheltered me for seventeen years. Though I had a substantial six-month writing contract, I could not predict what lay in store for me beyond that time.

My defenses were down. I felt vulnerable, like a lobster without its shell. It seemed to be a good time to find out who my true friends were. The man I visited on that spring day was someone I'd known for fifteen years. We had not been as close as either of us might have liked, but I had always suspected we had a lot in common. What I knew about him was more important: that he was a person who possessed a remarkable wisdom and generosity of spirit and that he dispensed these with compassion and genuine good will.

That friend was Jeff Patnaude, the author of this book. Over the course of the morning, he shared some of the milestones of his own journey, which was remarkably similar to the path I was just beginning. Jeff described the watershed that had changed the course of his own life. Four years before, he, too, had left a career in institutional religion—the Episcopal priesthood—that had become an ordeal of servitude rather than a career of service. He had bid an anguished good-bye to a long-term marriage, sacrificed an eighteen-room house in Shaker Heights, Ohio, and had returned to California with little more than a grandfather clock (one that chimed every hour as we conversed), his clothes, and a small store of cash. After some serious introspection and the guidance of a trusted mentor, Jeff decided to explore his inner resources. There he would discover a strong foundation for a new life: the balancing of the body, mind, and spirit and—to paraphrase an expression often used by members of the Dominican order—"sharing with others the fruits of his contemplation."

That mentor reminded Jeff—often—that it was more important to practice deep principles than just to discover them; rather like the difference between reading a seed catalog and cultivating ripe tomatoes in your garden. Thus, from the beginning, Jeff was resolved to do something concrete with the strengths his inner inventory had revealed.

Jeff had a strong background in public speaking, and, as a priest, he had worked for years with prominent business leaders, helping them to make ethically sound choices in workplaces that sometimes seemed to place a low value on integrity. Jeff's idea was to build a human resource consulting firm that would not only train employees in necessary business skills, but would offer leadership development programs that would bridge the gap between the worlds of business and spirituality.

Jeff's dream of creating a revolutionary business and values consulting firm involved many steps. Each one carried its own lesson; none was without cost. Collectively, these steps resembled a journey along the sinuous path of a labyrinth: Before arriving at the maze's center, Jeff would veer ever closer to the center, yet he had to summon the courage to turn in unexpected directions. In Jeff's new career, that "center" meant creating a year-long seminar for the evolution of business leaders, who themselves would make a similar journey. Along the way, these corporate executives would discover their own inner resources, applying their new insights to the daily challenges of their professional lives with new effectiveness, creativity, and power.

The seminar was entitled EAGLES, an acronym that stands for Executives Affirming Greatness in Leadership, Excellence, and Spirit. During our conversation that March day, we talked about how Jeff had refined his EAGLES seminar over a period of three years. Word had gotten out about the value of this unusual program, and demand for it was swelling. He had invited experts from many fields—business, academia, public speaking, counseling, the aesthetic and healing arts—to share in the direction of the seminar and provide a unique and rich experience for the participants. By this juncture, Jeff had also begun to build a community of associates—the Patnaude Group—who would teach by example the essentials of balanced leadership for all those enmeshed in the maze of today's business world.

The powerful impression Jeff Patnaude makes on corporate and societal leaders cannot be separated from his dynamic personal presence. One cannot walk away from his seminars without a clear and lasting memory of his physical energy and amiable manner. Jeff is a rare example of a man who can jest about himself and yet maintain a healthy sense of self-appreciation and dignity. Schooled by years of pulpit presence, Jeff has stripped away the puffed-up piety of many Sunday sermons and distilled the essential and best part of that oratorical tradition. His calm cadence and inventive use of parables humanize abstract concepts; he puts ancient principles in a contemporary light so that these concepts fit into—and strengthen—the lives of executive leaders from dozens of American corporations.

When it comes to assessing the needs, talents, and potential of others, Jeff's own intuition and insight are uncannily accurate. These qualities are coupled with an uncommon business acumen and a fascination with the challenges of contemporary corporate life. Whether a corporation is forming or reinventing an image of itself, Jeff has much to offer in helping to shape that process.

As we talked, Jeff told me of his belief in a "law of abundance"—that there is enough in the universe for all of us to receive what we need. His belief was joined to a conviction that business as an institution had both the power and the responsibility to create abundance for an ever greater number of people in the world. Jeff Patnaude's own story of professional and personal trial and success is a testimony to the idea that authentic leadership, based on the practices of inner management, can help bring the ideal of abundance more fully into being.

That morning the idea emerged for a book that would communicate to a business readership both the EAGLES concepts
and the experience of the labyrinthine journey of leadership.
You now hold the result in your hands. I am glad to have witnessed its inception and know you will find it of value in your
business and personal life.

John R. Archer, Ph.D.
New Haven, Connecticut
July 30, 1995

ROADMAP FOR THE MAZE

BUSINESS, MORE THAN ANY OTHER organizational force, has the power to change the planet. The influence of business leaders upon modern society is arguably the strongest of any institution—more direct than the educational system, more effective than political institutions, and more tangible than religious ones—because business leaders have both the ability and the authority to determine the nature of the environment in which people live and work.

Most executives are not insensitive to that fact—or to the responsibility it entails. They are simply not fully aware of their calling to serve as the architects of transformation.

This roadmap will lay out the maze's route, which is the course that this book will lead you through. No leader can effectively lead until he or she has charted the hidden domain of the inner self. First we'll look at examples of leadership and then we'll explore how the maze can bring forth inner qualities that are key to the authentic leader.

Leadership in Business

Leadership is the highest spiritual calling, and as business leaders, we cannot be of service to humankind until we can manage the business of our whole self, including the resources of spirit that lie within each of us. In fact, this is where leaders must begin—by practicing inner resource management.

We spend more time at work than anywhere else. Corporations become our new tribe, if not our family, and the ex-

ternal work environment becomes a reflection of our inner lives.
Far too often, businesses worship performance, productivity,
and profit and attempt to create environments that exact those
things in quantity from employees. The outstanding leader, however, seeks also to promote the inner qualities of commitment,
creativity, and responsibility within the heart of the worker.

Most leadership training programs focus on external skills
for doing things better or achieving more, rather than empha-
sizing the dimension of self-discovery. The training done by
most companies doesn't take into account that when people are
inspired by vision and purpose, their whole being becomes
committed to excellence.

Business observers, such as George Washington University's Peter Vaill, professor of human systems, think of corporate executives today as river runners caught in interminable
white water: Domestic and foreign competitors jostle many
companies until they threaten to capsize or run aground.
Changes in course occur frequently and at a dizzying speed
with new technology causing product lines to become obsolete
in microseconds. Increasingly, companies must redesign the
boat itself—perhaps cutting space, or paring down to a skele-
ton crew. More and more often, veteran oarsmen find themselves out on their own, paddling their own craft, whether by
choice or a twist of fate. For these people, and for veteran river
pilots who need to keep hold of all their resources to stay on
course, this book will provide a helpful resource.

Examples of Great Leadership

Throughout the history of humankind, truly great leaders have
discovered an inner treasury of resources and gifts that enabled
them to confront complex, seemingly insurmountable challenges.
Inspired by the power to serve, the able leader is not weighted
down by fear or indecision, but moves through the world with
ease and communicates with lucidity. Such leaders draw greatness out of others and assemble forces to serve a vision.

Let's consider the example of Jesus as a leader, quite apart
from his religious significance. We discover a young man who,

in three short years, transformed the traditional society he lived in. Teaching was his life's work and his constant passion. He showed people that all they ever needed lay within them, imparting this great lesson through simple stories adorned with humor, wit, emotional force, and an almost playful ease. His effect on the people of his time was electric. Inspiring both devotion and ferocious animosity, he never wavered from his vision in spite of death threats. Furthermore, he knew how to delegate responsibility for his message and purpose to those he mentored, so that even after his death, his reputation as a leader and teacher did not diminish, but expanded to cover the globe.

Winston Churchill should serve as another historical mentor to the modern business world. As a leader, he showed an extraordinary capacity to take criticism from the English electorate. At one time all but disregarded by his country, he reemerged as a tenacious fighter. Possessing a phenomenal grasp of world events, he stood firm at a time of grave national crisis, inspiring his compatriots, who were poised on the threshold of despair, with a clear vision of hope. Passionate and powerful, Churchill, when his needful time had passed, was able to step away from public life with dignity and grace.

Leaders such as these exist today as well. They know the value of work, yet they realize that people are so much more than the sum of what they do. Leaders enrich, inspire, and transform the workplace. When they speak, it is as if the room has expanded, making more oxygen available for everyone. Clearly themselves, rather than just another anxious ego, they are both whole and wholly present. In the pages that follow, you'll meet some people who I believe carry the qualities of great leadership. More importantly, you will enhance your ability to discover and define those qualities in yourself.

Qualities of Authentic Leadership

The qualities that serve as components for this book are essential elements for enlightened leadership. This book is written for people who want to make inner values an intentional part of their own leadership and management style. These concepts may have a particular meaning for women in the business world, many of whom have been consistently open to co-creating. It is my hope that exploration of the connection between spirituality and leadership will have a unique appeal and break new ground for business texts that take into account the whole person (not just the external personality, but also the hidden inner self and its resources).

The art of leading well is actually synonymous with being deeply human and fully alive. Few leaders set out to be leaders. Instead, they set out to lead an authentic, vital life, expressing their own lives fully. When that expression resonates with others, they become leaders.

How do we go about living a life fully expressed—the prerequisite for leadership? The answer is quite simple. We must first learn to become ourselves. In the inward journey to the true self, it is essential to learn to withhold nothing and be open to everything.

The Meaning of the Maze

> Not I—not anyone else, can travel
> that road for you. You must travel it
> for yourself.
>
> WALT WHITMAN,
> "SONG OF MYSELF"

Life can feel like a maze. For some leaders, that maze summons them to a quest: Solving problems and achieving the impossible are exhilarating challenges. To others, life's labyrinth is a trap of frustrating complexity, fraught with barriers and confusing turns that break the spirit of the timid traveler.

Whatever our perception, the maze is a metaphor for our times in a world searching for a new way to be. The destiny of humankind can be an aimless meandering path, or an intentional journey, rich in meaning and purpose. Which interpretation we embrace is a matter of our own choice.

Chartres Cathedral Labyrinth: A unicursal maze that leads the traveler along a single meandering path from the entrance to the center and then out again. Built into the floor of the cathedral, this three-circuit labyrinth has seven 180-degree turns and covers an area forty feet in diameter.

Human societies the world over have created labyrinths and other types of mazes. Along with the well-known megalithic labyrinths in Spain, the Celts and Minoans, Etruscans and Babylonians also invented their own versions. Archeologists have discovered classical Roman and Greek labyrinths, and spiral mazes in New Zealand and Vietnam. A labyrinth in Val Camonica, Italy, was carved into stone between 1000 and 1800 B.C. The Pharaoh Amenemhat III built a huge maze in 1795 B.C. composed of between 1,500 and 3,000 rooms above ground and 1,500 rooms beneath the earth. Travelers through this maze had literally hundreds of decisions to make.

*Scandinavian Lindbacke: seven-circuit labyrinth built
with rocks on the edge of the Baltic Sea.*

Images of the labyrinth have appeared in various forms in
many cultures and religions over the past 4,000 years, from the
Celts to the Hopis, in Tibetan Buddhism and Jewish mysticism,
in China, in Scandinavia, in Ireland, in Turkey, in Africa.
Mazes have been carved in cliffs of stone, woven into baskets,
laid out in pebbles, tiled on the floors of cathedrals, and cut
into the living turf.

These enigmatic structures vary widely in purpose and design. Some are puzzles with pathways meant to confuse,
branching off and leading to dead ends. Some contain high
walls that never allow the traveler to see where they are, in
which one can get lost and even perish. This type of maze is a
puzzle designed to trick the user, a hostile environment that
competes with the traveler for victory.

*Hopi Indian "Mother Earth" symbol, nearly identical
to the labyrinth image embossed on the Knossos coin.*

The Christian labyrinth design began appearing in European churches around the eighth century. Some say that the rose-petal center symbolizes the Virgin Mary; the six petals, the six days of creation.

A metaphor for the enigma of life's purpose, mazes have attracted religious pilgrims who have walked them in search of meaning. At one time a substitute for a pilgrimage to Jerusalem, the journey through the labyrinth remains the metaphor for the larger pilgrimage of life: a tortuous path that leads over and over to almost the same spot. Only through patience and persistence does the traveler attain the center, and the way out is as important as the way in. In some real-life mazes, the path is so narrow that it must be walked alone, allowing no companion or guide other than intuition.

Although not used for its original purpose as a pilgrim's path for the last 350 years, the labyrinth is becoming more widely known as it reemerges as a spiritual tool for today's leadership.

The model of the labyrinth in this book is a circular one based on one of the world's best known representations, the labyrinth at Chartres Cathedral, west of Paris. Built by Benedictine monks 800 years ago, the cream-colored stones of this great circular maze cover an area forty feet in diameter. Located in the central nave of this ancient church and clearly visible against its dark gray pavement, the labyrinth's dimensions correspond exactly to those of the rose window in the west portal. The stones trace a single meandering but unbranching path that leads from the entrance to the center and then out again. After reaching the center, the traveler continues along the same path to return to the beginning. There are no high walls or dead ends to confuse the user, but instead, a distinct path that serves as a guide for discovery.

The Rev. Lauren Artress, canon of Grace Cathedral in San Francisco and author of *Walking a Sacred Path*, describes the use of the labyrinth as a tool. "Whether you're Christian, Buddhist, Jewish, Muslim...It doesn't matter. The universal path of the labyrinth...sets it apart as a spiritual tool. The labyrinth does not engage our thinking minds. It invites our intuitive, pattern-seeking symbolic mind to come forth. It presents us with only one, but profound choice. To enter a labyrinth is to choose to walk a spiritual path."

The Greek philosopher Heracleitus described the labyrinth this way:

> Grasping: wholes and not wholes
> convergent divergent, consonant dissonant
> from all things one from one thing all.

The labyrinth is a symbol of an intangible process of assimilating the opposites: the presence of obstacles during the journey inward, and absence of obstacles on the journey outward, a construction of form and of emptiness. When the traveler is willing to embrace this paradox, he or she simultaneously seeks the heart of the void and the interconnectedness of all things. Using his or her imagination, the leader can travel this sacred path anytime, anywhere, and use it both as a way of spirit and a tool for business.

Phase I: The Journey Inward

> Go, not knowing where; bring, not
> knowing what; the path is long, the
> way unknown; the hero knows not
> how to arrive there by himself.
>
> RUSSIAN FOLK SAYING

As the traveler approaches the entrance to the maze, it is wise to be aware of the challenge ahead, for the journey within is a dangerous one. The path is not only circuitous and teeming with confusing options, but full of shadows and dragons that protect the treasure of the center. As with all mythological quests, the warrior must overcome the barriers preventing her or him from triumphing.

To successfully journey to the labyrinth's center, the seeker must travel lightly. Heavy thoughts, fears, and the weight of concern will only serve as additional barriers to achieving the goal. We are all familiar with the simplification process involved in moving to a new home. The move requires a weeding out of items no longer considered crucial. This process is similar to the process of the journey inward, as we dispose of unnecessary items that can become burdensome. Self-doubt, fear, misguided perception, and childhood wounds can become obstacles to clarity. On the journey inward, we relinquish them.

Phase II: The Center of the Maze

Here, in the center of the labyrinth, a treasure awaits the seeker. At the maze's center is the paradox of the intangible, a place of both mystery and knowledge. It is here that the seeker can experience the power of feeling a void of time and space, yet also feel a connection with every aspect of life. As a result of this emptying and simplification process, the knots of former beliefs become unraveled and the heart and mind have room to receive the new guest, wisdom.

Achieving one's goal usually requires action. But what is action? Some decisions require inaction or a period of waiting for the right time. Those, too, are conscious decisions.

Tax professional Charleen Daefield benefited from time spent in the center of the maze. Long burdened by a great dissatisfaction with her work, she entered into a lengthy period of reflection—the place of center—to determine why she was so unhappy. Daefield realized that she was, at heart, a "completer/finisher" personality who derived her greatest satisfaction from doing a job well and completing tasks. But bookkeeping—which at the time made up fifty percent of her business—was a never-ending process. The other half of her business, preparing taxes, afforded her the opportunity to do what she does best. Consequently, she farmed out her bookkeeping work to a thorough and efficient firm, and is now thrilled with her work and her growing business.

Presenting itself often in the form of intuitive knowing, a vision can be revealed to the traveler. To the unencumbered seeker, the clarity and comprehension gained at the center will lead to application. The heart, emboldened by the mind, is ready to begin the final phase, the journey outward.

Phase III: The Journey Outward

It is in the third phase that the labyrinth becomes an integrative vehicle for authentic leadership. The simplification during the journey inward has enormous power that invites wisdom to shelter within the deepest levels of our consciousness for one reason alone—to act.

For the leader—of a nation or in the world of business—the highest order of action in life is service. That leader becomes a vehicle of healing and wholeness for others. All true visions that come from the maze's center will, in some way, lead us to action. Thus, during the journey outward the leader resolves to act on behalf of the common good.

APPLICATION

How can the labyrinth—an instrument of mythology—apply to business? How can the maze's journey serve as a template to the leader who is faced with multiple decisions daily?

Debbie Fields, founder of Mrs. Fields Cookies, employs thousands of people and brings in a gross income in excess of $118 million annually (not including the income of the almost 400 franchise stores). Twenty years ago she had a vision of creating freshly baked, high quality cookies for the public. To test the market, she gave away her baked goods to passersby near her first store in Palo Alto, California. Instinctively following the maze's template, Fields was able to surmount natural barriers, such as the fear of rejection and failure, to promote her idea; she bypassed the threat of larger and more powerful competitors by producing a uniquely superior product. Finally, she put her idea into action with her cookie shops, of which there are now 700 spread throughout the U.S. and ten other nations.

The primary role of the leader is to provide vision for the organization. Whereas managers employ the many aspects of that vision, the leader provides the original image. How can organizations know where they are going if they do not have a vision as to which direction is the right one? And how do we determine what is the "right direction"? To do so, the authentic leader must:

△ Confront the barriers that stand guard over clarity
△ Take the necessary time to seek a wisdom beyond
   the limitations of ego or fear
△ Stand behind a solid vision in spite of dissension

That is the strength of the maze's three part process.

I led a conference on strategic vision some years ago with members of a high-tech corporation, using the first two phases of the maze—the journey inward and the center—as a foundation for our work. The company had a goal: to produce a mission statement and strategic plan in only two days. I decided to allot the whole first day to the journey inward. The participants arrived at the first off-site session with pads, pencils, and a desire to complete this task as quickly as possible. Told that they would need no materials other than themselves, they looked at me as if I were taking away their security blankets. When I began by teaching them a deep-breathing, quieting technique that they were to practice throughout our two days together, many were convinced that they had actually arrived at the wrong conference center. The day ensued with solitary walks, tai chi, journal-writing, naps, play time, and reflection about the obstacles—lack of focus, differences in ideas, conflict with other team members—they would need to remove before we could begin. Some were confused; many grumbled, wondering aloud when they were going to "get to work."

The next morning, rested, refreshed, and clearer in thought, we moved to the place of center. Quite rapidly, they tapped into another level of thinking and assembled a mission statement and strategic plan before lunch. Astounded by the clarity of thinking and speed of the process, the team departed five hours early, having achieved their goals.

The Foundation: Taking Time

A strong vision requires a natural time for gestation and deep roots if it is to weather change. One summer I planted a flower garden in a packed-soil plot that had been unattended for many years. Tilling the rock-hard ground proved a major undertaking, and so, frustrated, I loosened it just enough to plant. At first the flowers seemed to do well, bringing lively color to a lifeless garden. By mid-July however, all the blossoms had wilted, and many died. Their shallow roots provided inadequate support in ground not prepared thoroughly enough. Once the intense heat of the summer sun became constant, the plants had no staying power. Had I taken the time to mulch, creating a fertile bed, or to till, allowing the roots to reach a deeper level, a robust garden might well have flourished all season. Instead, time and money were wasted.

Months later, in the same area, I planted a rosebush given to me by a very close friend. Wanting it to bloom for years to come, I dug a deep hole and also added soil conditioner to prepare the spot for the young plant. The rosebush began to thrive immediately, producing six perfect roses during its first season. The second year, forty bloomed. From this experience I learned a most useful and important fact: there is no substitute for taking the time necessary to prepare the foundation for the desired goal. With this idea in mind, we begin the journey toward inner management.

DISCIPLINES FOR MASTERY

ANY MASTER OF THE MARTIAL ARTS spends years disciplining mind, body, and spirit. Great athletes in training learn to draw from the center of these fundamental sources, as does any professional performer. To consummate the highest of callings, powerful leaders must also master three specific disciplines: Attentiveness, Release, and Intention. We must practice these disciplines with a balanced approach. As with a three-legged stool, each leg is essential; if any one of them is removed, the stool will collapse. When this sturdy triad holds together, however, it forms one of the strongest structural supports known.

Resisting Old Patterns

Is it easy to master these disciplines? Many leaders who participate in traditional skill-building seminars return to their companies full of enthusiasm, eager to apply the new tools to the workplace. Yet within days, many return to old patterns of management.

THE DILETTANTE

The manager I characterize as the Dilettante will enthusiastically embrace a particular practice in the beginning. Soon, however, his zeal will wane, and the idea be retired to the shelf, like an unread book. Health clubs depend on this capriciousness for their financial survival. They know that such subscribers will disappear soon after securing a membership, making room for the next capricious personality.

THE ADDICTIVE-OBSESSIVE

The Addictive-Obsessive will become consumed by the discipline, making the practice her sole priority, to the exclusion of all other responsibilities. Like the stray whale that mysteriously leaves its deep ocean birthplace to swim toward eventual destruction in a shallow, narrow bay, the Addictive-Obsessive will slowly self-destruct from the choking confines of her own mind.

THE WEEKEND WARRIOR

The Weekend Warrior proclaims the importance of self-discipline but only takes the time to practice it away from the workplace. The frustrated CEO who plays weekend racquetball with a vengeance in an attempt to work off a week's worth of stress is a perfect example. Stress reduction requires daily attention, not an occasional commitment.

Incorporating a balanced, daily approach is both the goal and practice of the master.

Attentiveness:
The Discipline of the Journey Inward

As the poet-philosopher Lao-tzu wrote in the Tao Te Ching, "A journey of three thousand miles begins with a single step." Awakening is the first step in our inner journey.

We can begin the path of a life fully expressed only when we are truly awake. To cultivate attentiveness, I often have members of seminar groups choose a wooden match from a box and spend five minutes silently paying attention to its uniqueness. When the matches are collected, participants can still easily identify their match, having become aware of every tiny detail. The lesson is simple: When we pay attention, we begin to see that which can so easily disappear in the camouflage of business.

One of the secrets of developing the discipline of attentiveness is to remain in the present. Certainly we learn from the past, but the seeds of the future are unfolding in the present. If we pay attention, we will see them. Attentiveness deepens as we progress along the maze's path. You'll find that the more you hone this discipline, the sharper and more fully alive you'll be. Like a fine wine, this practice improves with time.

ATTENTIVENESS OF MIND

The mind can be our advocate or our adversary. It can deride us into succeeding at any cost, or it can guide us along a path of integrity. The mind can embrace pretense or truth. It is the harbinger of wisdom.

Learning to distinguish between truth and illusion comes through mindfulness. Meditation, practiced daily, harnesses the leader's capacity for awareness of her or his body, mind, and the workplace itself. Such mindfulness allows the leader to filter through the dissonance of the work environment and, later, to quietly put inner wisdom into action.

In the EAGLES seminars, we teach leaders an exercise in which each breath reminds the practitioner to remain attentive. We encourage participants to place adhesive-backed colored dots on frequently used objects such as telephones, computers, or a wristwatch. Every time the person sees the dots, she or he is reminded to take a breath and refocus on her or his wise inner voice.

The gentle nudges of our intuition are significant signposts along the path of the labyrinth, and we train leaders to pay attention to them. In a seminar last year, one corporate consultant told a story that illustrates why. Several weeks before, she had set out to buy handles for kitchen cabinets in her home. Oddly, as she drove within two blocks of the hardware store where she'd planned to shop, her intuition urged her to turn around and head in the opposite direction. Driving past a furniture store she had never seen before, she entered to look for the handles. In the course of finding them, she met a man who would become an extraordinarily valuable business contact in Los Angeles—exactly the connection she needed to expand her company. To many people, this kind of incident seems doubtful or a fluke. Yet as we learn to utilize our intuition, such helpful flashes become more and more common.

ATTENTIVENESS TO BODY

When in danger, the body instantly prepares itself for the ancient response of fleeing or fighting. Its systems work at speeds ranging from lightning-quick to lethargic, depending on what is required. One of the most complex art forms in creation, the human body works relentlessly on behalf of the traveler. Without the body, we cannot fully sense the challenges of the maze nor confront the dragons that reside within. Caring for it is our ongoing challenge and, ultimately, our privilege.

Exercise and good nutrition are the simplest ways to pay attention to this deserving creation. Sluggishness can be transformed into bursts of creative energy simply by working muscles and systems that thrive on being challenged. If you revere the vehicle that houses our passion, it will meet the demands of leadership.

In the workplace, as leaders become more attentive to the needs of their own bodies, they will assist in creating healthier work climates for all who labor on behalf of their vision.

ATTENTIVENESS TO SPIRIT

Our consulting work continually reminds managers that the climate of the workplace is a direct result of their behavior, which in turn is a result of their motives and what they value. If their values are less than honorable, then the environment can become a mire. In a healthy workplace, a leader acts as a beacon of light. Spirit powers that beacon.

Like the Hebrew word *ruah*, and the Greek *pneuma*, the Latin root of the word for spirit gave birth to the term for breath—something we have when we are alive and don't have when we are dead. Spirit, then, has to do with living life in fullness and expressing the power of the life that lives within us. When we are unusually vital, we communicate a life so rich that it can affect the lives of others. Our breath can literally breathe new life into those in need of resuscitation. The great leader fills the room with what feels like oxygen. Those who experience the power are "in-spired," or, literally, infused with spirit.

In my set of beliefs, the source of spirit is God, as God is spirit. Rather than the antiquated image of an old man with a beard—an image that remains the primary one in Western minds—God is the essence of all creativity and passion, delicious in character and devoted in purpose; the source of all creation gives breath to all things. Desiring and learning to tap that inexhaustible breath is one of life's greatest pleasures. With it, we pass along to others what we have received.

Release: The Discipline of Center

One of the most remarkable tenets of the center is the most difficult of life's lessons: the universe has its own plan and is moving toward its own intended destiny. Similarly, in business, we can lead, but cannot control other people's every action. As leaders, the moment we realize that, we learn to release the desire to be in charge of everything. When we do, our lives and workplace become receptive to the abundance of resources, ideas, and energy that the universe freely provides.

One facet of letting go and trusting forces beyond our control is captured in the following story: A trapeze artist practiced her art on a high wire over a canyon a thousand feet deep.

One day a wanderer came to the edge of the precipice where the artist was rehearsing. The performer greeted the visitor and asked him if he thought it was possible for her to cross the wire blindfolded, without falling. The wanderer, impressed by the talent of the artist, responded affirmatively, and indeed, the artist performed the feat. The artist then asked if the hiker thought it possible to balance on the wire on one finger. Although this was a far more difficult act, the wanderer's response again encouraged the artist to successfully accomplish the act. Then the artist came back with a wheelbarrow and asked the hiker if he thought she could successfully cross the thousand-foot drop pushing the wheelbarrow. The wanderer, now fully confident in the ability of this great performer again replied in the affirmative.

"Good," said the artist, "get in."

The center of the labyrinth requires a similar demonstration of faith. In the midst of the quest, a precipice can appear and provide the leader with a mystical encounter with wisdom far beyond normal consciousness—but the leader can only have that encounter if he or she takes the next step, trusts in intuition, and gets in. Letting go of a sense of control is the hardest human act to perform, yet it is a critical part of the process of illumination. We cannot be receptive if we stand unmoving at that precipice, letting fear prevent us from moving forward. When we let go, we become fertile ground to receive the seeds of wisdom.

Intention:
The Discipline of the Journey Outward

Having a desire to change is not enough to create change. If we try obsessively to achieve something, we are already yielding to defeat. If we intend to accomplish a task, we are partway there. Because each of our intentions—whether anger, hate, love, or understanding—sets energy in motion, we must be mindful of what we project. Intention is more than desire; it is an act of the will.

I coached a CEO whom I believed intended to fail so that he could leave a position that he loathed. He insisted that his intention was to succeed and prove his worth. Although he created the illusion of hard work and determination, he did everything possible to sabotage himself. As he limped toward the finish line, he failed miserably in his goal and was relieved of his job. He felt that he had failed as he did not achieve that which he intended. I believe he achieved exactly what he intended and that his subconscious mind won the battle over his conscious intention.

Learning the clarity of our intentions is a critical step for achieving the right action. When we are clear, we become a vehicle for a passion. It is an energy that is very evident. Unlike the CEO just described whose vision remained clouded in a fog, the leader with clear vision and intention is like a laser, able to cut through the obstacles on the path of action. The dragons of the maze are no match for the traveler who carries his own light source and forges ahead in spite of the barriers. Intentions, therefore, are power. They are a source of energy as they shape our physical reality.

If the journey outward is to be effective in utilizing the plan that has come from the wisdom of center, the planned action must not be desired, but intended.

Simple Labyrinth: Basic classical labyrinth constructed around the four points of a cross.

THE JOURNEY INWARD

A Way of Being

PURPOSE:
To enter into oneself to discover an individual
foundation for wise and balanced leadership.
During this phase the leader confronts and
defeats the dragons, or obstacles,
to the journey inward.

DISCIPLINE FOR MASTERY:
Attentiveness

PRACTICES OF
INNER MANAGEMENT:
• Journey • Choice
• Balance

Experience has given me one certainty—and that is that consciousness precedes being and not the other way around. For this reason, the salvation of the world lies nowhere else than in the human heart, in the human power to reflect and in human responsibility. Without a global revolution in the sphere of human consciousness, nothing will change for the better in the sphere of our being as humans.

VACLAV HAVEL, PRESIDENT OF CZECHOSLOVAKIA
SPEECH TO THE UNITED STATES CONGRESS, 1990

We begin the journey through the labyrinth by descending into the realm of the inner self, through the first triad of leadership practices. Masterfully attentive, conscious of the dangers, the awakened traveler enters, knowing the first and only stop is at the place of center, a long way ahead. Our understanding of leadership is discovered in the exploration, adventure, and learning along the path before us. All are ways for us to take another step toward our intended destiny, to serve.

Certainly, the journey's most consistent characteristic is the confrontation with constant change, and the necessity to make choices at every turn of the maze. Choice, therefore, lies near the heart of this evolutionary process, as we participate in shaping the world.

No society has been as consistently marked by change as our own; technology and globalization have turned the world into a vast kaleidoscope of shifting patterns. Not only does this increase choices and decisions, it also renders the journey precarious. In an age known for its lack of stability, discovering a point of balance within ourselves is an essential practice. The call for leaders to seek a balance of body, mind, and spirit is not just an optional quest, like a casual desire for more education, stronger faith, or a trimmer body. It is necessary for human well-being. Balance carries individual and collective implications that can shape personal goals and influence corporate structure.

Nevertheless, it is easy to lose hope as the familiar structures of the past give way to changing realities in the present. One lesson the journey teaches us is to see hope in the future, even when it may seem as if the world as we know it is disintegrating. The beauty of the labyrinth is that the seeker is always able to see the center—though it may be distant—from its curving paths. The architects of the world's future are those who find the courage to face the prospect that the future will unfold, giving birth to renewal.

As long as we remain focused on the journey, open to choice, and poised to balance the change that is part of life itself, we and the organizations we lead will grow vital, connected by strong ties to the source of human spirit.

It is crucial for a company's health to envision itself on a path toward a well-considered, long-term purpose that incorporates a desire not only for profit, but to contribute back to the community and the workplace, to benefit both shareholders and employees. Company leaders must define not only the products they want to market, but the legacy they wish to leave to the world. Perceiving company members as being on a journey together, joining and sharing their individual stories like pilgrims in Chaucer's *Canterbury Tales* is essential for determining that deeper purpose.

1 JOURNEY

> I think of journey as a search. We
> search for a self to be, we search
> for other selves to love, we search
> for work.
>
> FREDERICK BUECHNER,
> *SACRED JOURNEY*

IT IS JANUARY, AND PACIFIC STORMS lash the coast of California with the regularity of a metronome. Rain falls steadily on a small cluster of redwood buildings at a retreat located just south of the San Francisco Bay. In a comfortable conference room eight men and four women sit holding soft leather binders bearing the image of a majestic eagle in flight.

All the participants are proven leaders—CEO's, professionals, entrepreneurs—whose talent and vision have earned them success as the world measures it. Somehow, each of them had become aware that outward accomplishments were not enough. "I'm at the pinnacle of my career. I've made all the money I'll ever need. I'm searching for something more," said one CEO, speaking for many in the group. Each of them wanted something more lasting than financial reward, more substantial than praise or professional standing. They each came to believe that what they sought lay on another path, one that began within. It is this awareness that calls this particular group to meet on a damp winter evening, and their time together will occupy an important place in their life and work for the better part of a year.

The following chapters of this book describe the practices of inner management explored by business leaders in EAGLES seminars over the last five years. Many of the vignettes depicting "leadership from the inside out" are taken directly from the experiences these leaders had in the EAGLES seminars. Each of the participants walked a path that was in some way a labyrinth, replete with struggling, suffering, joy and sorrow, trial and error. As we know, the labyrinth holds no security from catastrophe; yet if we remain safe, refusing to risk new experiences, we forfeit the chance for independence and for true consciousness.

The Journey's Challenge

In a sense, corporate systems are projections of the individuals who guide them. The leader's strengths become strengths for the system, just as dysfunctional aspects are the seeds for its problems. Such personal characteristics as denial, confusion, self-centeredness, dishonesty, and perfectionism are reflected in abusive and insensitive policies, a climate of fear, and ethical deterioration.

In my work, I have encountered many leaders who cannot pass through the essential change required to reach the center of the maze and whose progress is halted. For some, the demand to relinquish control is too frightening, or they may regard the inner life as illusory, a waste of time. They have risen to power by operating competently and effectively in the external world, at the cost of internal awareness.

We commonly assume that chief executives are necessarily strong, charismatic, decisive and confident, always in control, and fearless in asserting their will within the organization. The truth is that they are often filled with doubts about their ability to perform to such a high standard. Those doubts might have arisen in the fragile time of childhood—brought about by caustic or critical remarks about a first painting, labeling innocence as stupidity, or forcing a child to be responsible for an adult's rage or pain. These are not, sad to say, rare experiences. Virtually all of us bear the wounds of such messages, and successful executives are not an exempt class. Self-doubt creates an uncertain picture of who we are, which in turn often obscures the image of who we can be.

St. Thomas Aquinas said that despair is the first step in the birth of a spiritual life. In today's world, we are certainly poised on the threshold of despair. Perhaps the despair that afflicts our world will actually serve as a catalyst for creative change. Business leadership has the money, the power, and the opportunity to bring about this transformation.

The time has arrived for us to put our house in order, as E. F. Schumacher says in his book, *Small Is Beautiful*. "Everywhere," he writes, "people ask, 'What can I do?' The answer is as simple as it is disconcerting. The guidance for this work cannot be found in science or technology, the value of which utterly depends on the ends they serve. But it can still be found in the traditional wisdom of humankind."

Pathway to the Inner Frontier

Humankind's legacy has been to follow the path toward meaning, but sometimes we don't need to move great distances to find truth. Frequently, in fact, that inner treasure lies closer than we know. Indeed, we often resemble the South African farmer-adventurer who abandoned his home and family in a single-minded quest for diamonds. As the years passed, his relentless pursuit took its toll, and finally, he died. His body was sent home for burial, and there on his own farm, where neighbors opened the earth to dig his grave, their first spadefuls turned up the richest diamond lode ever discovered in South Africa! This true-life parable is useful to keep in mind as we journey inward together, exploring the practices of inner management that set the foundations for great leadership.

The Dragons in the Maze

In contrast to the traditional prototype of an unhindered rise to leadership, this labyrinth's path first takes the traveler downward and inward, and only then forward. Just as in the epic of Gilgamesh, the hero descends into the depths, encountering formidable monsters all along the way. Slaying the monsters isn't just about eliminating obstacles to reach the goal. In our

Labyrinthine tile from a French abbey.

adventure, the actual slaying of one's own demons is a major part of the journey. The frightening beasts and the dark shadows of the lower self become the springboards for the pursuit of our truest essence.

Along this path, three primary dragons lurk in the shadows, obstructing the goal of great leadership. They are fear, narcissism, and a poor sense of self. For a leader to reach her or his full potential, each beast must be uncovered, examined, and transformed before you proceed to the center of the maze.

Because most leaders have tremendous power to positively influence their environment, they often remain unaware of the equal power of the dark side and its insidious tendency to be projected through us onto those surrounding us. The executive director of a celebrated news corporation nearly drove his organization to ruin due to his inability to face his shadow side.

Seeing only his dedication and ideals for the corporation, he remained completely oblivious to the nepotism, pettiness, and anxiety he transferred to employees in a company that had been famous for its group spirit. By asking for his resignation, the board of directors rescued the firm just as it staggered on its last legs.

Indeed, many leaders avoid beginning the labyrinth's journey precisely because this first phase is so dangerous and difficult. To spend one's life manipulating institutions and corporations, the external world, is far easier than grappling with one's own soul. Yet great leadership comes from people who have made this downward journey.

To accomplish this challenging feat, the leader must first be awake and fully alert. Like a nighttime traveler attuned to every sound in the forest, the leader must be aware of all possibilities lurking in the shadows. For we can neither challenge nor transform what we cannot see.

Spiritual traditions all over the globe share the theme of awakening from a deep sleep to the light of illuminated consciousness. Buddhism defines enlightenment as the highest state of the mind. Jesus challenged his disciples to stay awake, watch and be humble. Because the dragons of the maze feed upon our inattentive, unconscious mind, our primary work becomes vigilance and the transformation of our own consciousness. Therefore, the first challenge along the labyrinthine path is to practice the discipline of attentiveness by being aware of all things.

THE DRAGON OF FEAR

The first and most formidable dragon that bars the way to the maze's illuminating center is the dragon of fear. This creature is the most powerful of all, and its omniscient presence spawns all other dragons. The dragon of fear reigns in the presence of rigidity and constriction, in contrast to the ease and openness we know when fear is absent. The fearful traveler of the maze can be consumed by its presence.

How can we recognize when this dragon lurks close by? We may notice it when we feel victimized by circumstances we believe are outside our realm of influence. If we see the universe as hostile and life as a battleground, then we'll disparage the security of group loyalties and regard everyone as a rival. It is this mentality that provokes relentless competition among corporations. Marketing is likened to guerrilla warfare and leadership styles are patterned after Attila the Hun. The dragon of fear infects us with the mentality of scarcity; we become obsessed with grabbing limited resources and dwindling reserves. In *Passages*, Gail Sheehy called the current ideology "a mix of personal survivalism, revivalism, and cynicism." Winners are heralded and losers are disdained, creating a survival-of-the-fittest mentality.

A hard-edged work environment characterized by control and rigidity, with many rules and procedures, lacerates company structure and fossilizes fluidity. A semiconductor equipment manufacturing company once invited me to observe staff reports given at a quarterly review. For three hours, I watched as staff members writhed in polite "dis-ease" in the presence of the CEO. The room was filled with tension, mistrust, and fear as each employee performed a kind of ritual dance around their boss. There was no give-and-take, no playful attitudes, no feeling of comfort. Instead I saw only the raw emotions generated by a desire to survive. The shadow side of that company's leadership permeated the system. I recommended building a climate of trust in part by mandating a retreat where employees could safely air grievances. The CEO rejected the notion entirely. The team lost three of its key members within the year.

Clinging to structure and rigid hierarchy as an antidote to fear results in a kind of militant fundamentalism that blocks the path to the maze's illuminating center. In the academic world, the dragon of fear often surfaces in relation to grading, the pressure to publish, and the intrigue surrounding tenure battles. Its power enslaves both student and professor. In places of worship, it may surface when the spiritual leaders' authority will not permit challenges to their role. Likewise, bureaucratic inertia often robs medical professionals of their ability to perform as humanely as they would like.

Whatever the catalyst, it is important for us to use our ability to sense fear at work. We all know its effects on our lives.

Perhaps we come from a family in which a parent manipulated others through mood or regulation of affection so that the entire family functioned solely to serve that person's needs. Perhaps we've known a teacher or an employer who created an atmosphere of such intense darkness that we felt compelled to leave an institution, realizing meaningful work could never be accomplished there. Whatever our training ground, we all have some form of fear built into our systems. Its primary forms are fear of intimacy, fear of failure, and fear of risk.

Fear of Intimacy

What we want most deeply is a total experience of being known and being accepted as we are. Beneath all the striving for money, power, recognition, and material things is a desire to be loved. But what prevents us personally from achieving the gift of intimacy is a fear of rejection. When we have experienced rejection, we become less willing to risk being vulnerable. With each rejection we protect ourselves with ever more isolation so as to not expose our interior self. Eventually, we may not even believe that we deserve positive attention and may feel discomfort when we receive it.

Because "how we do anything is how we do everything," we unfortunately bring our dysfunctional selves to work, creating systems that reflect our fears. Transforming the fear of getting too close is one of the greatest challenges of corporate cultures.

One of the more fear-ridden institutions of our present society is the banking industry. I grew up with a small town bank that assigned loans with your character and reputation as collateral. Nowadays, banks often ignore many small businesses seeking support for short-term business needs. I attribute the policies of the larger banks to an unwillingness to know their customers or to trust in their character and their vision. What people want most is to matter, to count, and to be recognized. When dispassionate and intimacy-avoiding systems declare "you are a nobody," fear of disclosure and vulnerability only increase. Fear combined with power creates even more fear.

I consult with a large computer manufacturing company

headquartered in both California and Texas. Hundreds of employees constantly travel between the two locations. A rather draconian company policy dictates that only corporate executives may stay in a particular hotel—the best hotel in the city—even if non-executives are willing to pay the difference in hotel costs from their own pockets. What kind of thinking establishes a policy preventing lower-level managers from enjoying the same pleasures as the executives? Are these leaders afraid of encounters in the lobby that might leave the public impression that they have a closer relationship with the non-executives than they desire?

I worked closely for one year with a Northern California firm whose top-level manager never once made eye contact with his staff at meetings. Even when he personally called for a meeting, he would start the gathering by demanding to know its purpose, in a tone suggesting that he had no time for such foolish wastes of time. He spoke in such a harsh, loud tone of voice that all staff members in attendance felt as if they were in a locked ward. In confidential meetings that are part of my consulting approach, his staff told me that his style was to try to undermine all their ideas and scare them into acquiescence. Meanwhile, his staff had developed their own strategy for survival. "Never," their strategy went, "schedule a meeting with him for less than 45 minutes." The explanation? "After the first ten minutes, he calms down enough so that your ideas can be heard and something productive can occur." Eventually the manager's style caught up with him. He was demoted from vice president to head of special projects, a solitary and far less prestigious position. Instead of a climate of joy, a climate of fear was generated by a man who is afraid to allow anyone to get too close.

Let's think back to the old paradigm of medical practice, when the physician was foremost a comforter who prescribed a treatment with the hope of a cure. Today, the order has reversed: "fixing" has become an obsession and most treatments focus on that end. "Comforter" is the last on the list of the physician's roles. The word compassion means "to suffer with"—a stance far too intimate for many physicians today. Technology is safe and provides an acceptable offering to the patient in need. However, the healing process requires far more than technology.

Physician and author Dean Ornish, in his work rediscovering the connection between mind and body, believes that intimacy is a path for physical healing. When our bodies experience acceptance and love, he believes, the climate for healing is greatly amplified. A recent study at Stanford University that tested rabbits with malignant tumors confirms this theory. Researchers injected two rows of caged rabbits with cancerous cells to observe the rate of tumor growth. For reasons not immediately obvious, the rabbits on the top row all grew malignant tumors at twice the rate as the rabbits on the bottom row. The possible explanation took some time to discern: The rabbits on the lower level were the only ones to receive the care and attention of the affectionate and very short attendant feeding them—which doctors believe contributed to those rabbits having more resistant immune systems. Too far above her eye level and reach, she was only able to feed the upper row of animals—not stroke and pet them.

If we let it, the dragon of fear can successfully eliminate one of the key elements of healing, for although what we seek most is to be fully known and loved for who we truly are, we shun intimacy due to fear.

Fear of Failure

Beginning in childhood, we are programmed to avoid failure at any cost. Sports, academics, and relationships are all fertile arenas for such programming. I have observed grade-school coaches literally screaming at eight-year-old children for losing a soccer game. We know parents who criticized the two B's on the report card rather than offer praise for the four A's. And early friendships became so significant that we often sacrificed our values in order to please others and receive approval.

Afraid to Speak

Fear of failing affects many aspects of our lives. In my role as a coach for public speakers, I work with people who are literally terrified about speaking before a group. A recent national poll revealed that when asked to name their greatest fear, fifty-three out of a hundred people say public speaking. (Ironically, only eighteen listed death as their greatest fear.) Why is this true? I suggest it is because of fear of failure. People in front of audiences are more interested in being successful than being memorable. The fear of looking foolish and appearing nervous or out of control is debilitating. If coached to focus on serving the audience with a message of substance and letting go of the need to succeed, the speaker can transform the intention behind the speaking experience; if the speaker puts the needs of the audience foremost and views the positive impact of her speech as her primary concern, she vanquishes the dragon of fear.

Afraid to Listen

The ability to listen is also affected by fear of failure. Do you notice that when someone speaks to you, often rather than listening you are thinking about what to say in response? The need to be quicker or wiser—even in the guise of wanting to be more helpful—prevents us from hearing. Fearful of failing, we become more interested in being successful than in being present. With such concerns distracting us we often miss what is being communicated.

In corporate life, fear of failure produces the "Don't make me look bad" syndrome. The leader driven by others' perceptions of her or him will keep a tight reign on any staff activities that could detract from the projected public image. A former chancellor of an internationally renowned university grew so obsessed with the fear of a blemished image that his fear eventually became prophecy. Repeatedly harassing his staff about "not making him look bad" resulted in his eventually being fired— ironically, for displaying such a poor image of leadership.

I always believed that Richard Nixon might have diminished the damage incurred by the Watergate scandal if he had only admitted his wrongdoing. However, the cover-up—his attempt not to look bad—created a swamp from which valuable objects— such as the honor of the presidency—became irretrievable.

Fear of Risk

If we have taken a risk, failed, and been reprimanded for our actions, like Pavlov's dogs, we quickly learn to behave differently in order to avoid the negative feedback.

Human creativity is boundless. New ideas are channeled through us constantly. Yet we often fail to act on these ideas, fearing "looking bad," or punishment. Imagine the wealth of important ideas that have been lost due to fear of failure. I meet people almost daily who live and work within the walls of a large corporation, yet their hearts call them to start their own businesses and follow their personal visions. Only the barrier of fear prevents them from moving but this barrier is dense enough to cause these people to sit in their cubicles dreaming about being elsewhere instead of taking action.

Embracing Failure

Many famous personalities had to overcome the fear of failing after other people's assurances—sometimes comic in retrospect—that they would not be successful. Lucille Ball, for example, was discouraged from pursuing comedy; she was told that no one would laugh at someone with red hair. Michael Jordan was kicked off his high school basketball team, told that he did not have enough talent. Picasso was ridiculed by his peers as having minimal artistic abilities, and Abraham Lincoln lost six elections before winning a public office. To discourage means to "dispirit," to actually depress the spirit within that calls us to risk taking the first step.

How rich our lives could be if we could embrace failure as one of the most significant ways to learn and to expand. As the Sufis have taught us, "When the student is ready, the teacher appears." When companies do everything possible to avoid either failing or acknowledging their failures, they are losing a great opportunity to learn from the failure and move forward with new wisdom.

Many of our clients are emerging companies that experience meteoric growth and try to maintain that flight pattern over the long run. When they encounter the inevitable big dipper, they attempt to work harder, faster, and smarter to overcome the change. What can be most important at this time is to celebrate their failures as a wake-up call to an important message. I encouraged members of one firm to gather every Friday at five to tip a glass of champagne to the meaningful failures of the week, analyze what the failures taught them, and determine the next move based on what they learned. If we can celebrate failure, we will not fear it and will be even more courageous in our risk-taking.

FEAR OF TRUTH

> Who is more foolish, the child
> afraid of the dark or the man afraid
> of the light?
>
> MAURICE FREEHILL

Lying: The Dragon Breathes

We seem to be living in the "post-truth" era. Deceit has become a mark of our civilization—not only the type of evil deceit in which someone benefits at the expense of others but the congenial deceit of social interaction that masquerades as civility. We may think that there are different gradations of lying, and that some lies are acceptable, but the reality is when we tell small untruths, we set up a deceitful foundation, and eventually, full-blown lies become commonplace.

Our national leaders have provided little positive modeling in recent years. Richard Nixon held the distinction of becoming the first president to resign because of his lies. George Bush escaped such disgrace, although he lied to the American public on a regular basis. In 1980, for example, he opposed Reaganomics, dubbing it "voodoo economics." Later, when tapped to join Reagan on the Republican ticket, Bush instantly transformed his opinion. He denied his former stand, insisting that he had never taken it. Later, NBC news would run a tape of his "voodoo economics" comment, followed immediately by his recorded denial of it. In 1988 he lied again about his knowledge of arms sales to Iran, then about his involvement with corrupt Panamanian president Manuel Noriega. In what was perhaps the best remembered case, after promising not to raise taxes in his famous "Read My Lips" speech, Bush went on to raise taxes 133 times. Indeed, when he left office, federal taxes were 476.4 billion dollars higher than in 1980. What do such lies do to the public morale?

The white lie, the "check is in the mail" syndrome can infect our daily lives to the point that we exaggerate, we avoid confrontation, we minimize, we spare people's feelings, and we feel justified in cheating large institutions. Gradually these habits have built an environment in which many people believe that lying is perfectly acceptable.

Ignoring obvious information can lead to another more subtle and insidious form of lying. Let me offer a graphic example. For a number of decades, high officials of the Roman Catholic Church served as a co-perpetrator with Father James Porter, a confessed pedophile who may have abused as many as one hundred children. Although complaints were filed in the 1960s, rather than suspend him temporarily, church authorities simply moved him from parish to parish, which only furthered his opportunities to abuse. After being treated for pedophilia in 1967, Porter returned to work and abused more children until he was finally relieved of his duties in 1968. Although no overt lie was told, the church's ignoring of the facts resulted in the wanton abuse of dozens of innocent children.

"Group-think"—a phenomenon in which individuals relinquish their own thoughts due to the pressure of a group ideology—allows key facts to be ignored because remaining loyal to the group becomes more important than the value of the truth. Two historical examples that show how group-think affected a major decision are the Japanese attack on Pearl Harbor and, more recently, the Challenger space shuttle disaster. In each case, available data was ignored. In the case of Pearl Harbor, it was evident by 1940 that Japan was preparing for massive military operation; with the space shuttle tragedy, evidence strongly suggested that the O-rings of the spaceship's booster rocket would not hold below a given temperature. In spite of warning signs, each group—the U.S. military and NASA space personnel—employed selective memory, then ignored the facts. Omission and denial contributed to the disasters that are now classic lessons from history.

Self-Delusion

> We lie loudest when we lie to
> ourselves.
>
> ERIC HOFFER

Self-delusion is probably the most common form of lying. We may use it as a survival mechanism in situations in which we feel we have no control. Or we may use it to justify harmful behavior we haven't the resolve to sacrifice. "I need this drink," "I only smoke because I am so stressed," "I don't have time to exercise," are phrases that may sound familiar. Corporations delude themselves when they believe that a money-making product, such as aerosol spray, is more important than the long-term damage the product does to the environment.

George Bernard Shaw said that one of the greatest punishments for lying is that "the liar cannot believe anyone else." The outcome of lying is that the inner self commits a crime against itself. It depletes our energy and erodes our inner life. When we tell the truth, we build the reservoir of inner strength that allows us to face the obstacles on the maze's path.

THE DRAGON OF POOR SELF-CONCEPT

> The greatest evil that can befall a
> man is that he should come to think
> ill of himself.
>
> JOHANN WOLFGANG VON GOETHE

The Patnaude Group offers a two-day course on improving one's self-concept. Considered a very "soft" issue in a very high-tech scene, its popularity has surprised even our staff members. Indeed, participants have repeatedly evaluated this training as one of the most significant learning events of their lives.

It is impossible to move to the level of great leadership if the leader internally believes that he or she is stupid, inept, or valueless. As basic as it may seem, self-concept is where we must begin to build a foundation for all else that will follow.

Negative feelings about ourselves come from bad experiences in which we accepted another person's perception that we are inadequate. How unfortunate this can be! Three years ago, a CEO of an important Silicon valley company attended the program. Although his professional accomplishments were widely recognized, at heart, he still felt that he was a failure. As a boy, his father had often told him that he would never amount to anything. Now, at the age of fifty-five, he continued to try to prove to his deceased father that he was a capable human being. This man headed a thriving company, had created jobs for thousands of people, and made millions of dollars, and yet he was miserable and insecure.

According to Freud's theory of symptomatic actions, behavior is caused by one's unconscious: a negative thought causes a negative response. Through the negative impulse sent to the unconscious, the thought manifests itself in a behavior. So, using a psychotherapeutic process called the "healing of memories," I led this executive toward a new image of his father. By removing the negative image of his father, the CEO was able to resume his work life in a joyful way.

In an EAGLES seminar one year, an enthusiastic but nervous participant raised her hand to ask a question. She started to speak, suddenly stopped, and began to cry. I soon realized she was crying with relief. She explained that by simply asking a question publicly, she had experienced a breakthrough in her own sense of self-worth. Through a flood of tears the woman recounted how, thirty-four years before, in grade school, she had asked a question in class. The teacher, short on patience and on wisdom, had snapped, "That's the stupidest question I have ever heard." From that incident until now, this forty-four-year-old woman had not asked a single question in public. It had taken her three decades to overcome the dragon of poor self-concept.

THE DRAGON OF NARCISSISM

The labyrinth's final dragon stands in marked contrast to the depreciated ego described above. This fabulously egocentric creature is the dragon of narcissism, which views itself at the center of the world. This shadow creature leaves no room either for divine energy or the creative input of other people. Its anti-Copernican view of the universe insists, "I must do everything myself if it is to be done well." Leaders who think this way refuse to delegate authority to subordinates, manipulate colleagues, and disempower those who seek to be part of a leadership team. They remain blind to the notion of leadership as a conduit connecting all of life.

The narcissistic influence has become endemic in the American workplace, and it leaves business leaders short on some rather important facts. When a Gallup poll asked employees if they would work more effectively if more involved in decisions related to their own work, an overwhelming 84 percent responded that they would. Although the number of employees now managing some aspect of their own work environment is on the increase, the percentages remain low; thus, the Narcissist stymies production itself, inadvertently as the case may be.

The term "narcissism" stems from the story of Narcissus, a youth who fell so deeply in love with his own image that he wasted away from unsatisfied desire. For Narcissus, the meaning of life became a reflection of his exterior image, which prevented him from discovering the beauty of his interior self, his truest self.

The Narcissist is a tragic character with an impoverished inner life. Haunted by anxiety, the Narcissist experiences no connection with the past and is fearful of the future. He is deeply antisocial and rejects cooperation and the benefit of teamwork. In fact, this character is fiercely competitive and distrusts even the assistance of others.

The reason that the maze's journey downward and inward is so challenging is because our culture has taught us that strong people are seldom afraid. The mentality of machismo has been one of the most successful anti-development crusades of all time. It has encouraged us to push fear from our consciousness and play roles that create disintegration among human beings. A whole person is not a role-player, but a complex, feeling, thinking, paradoxical being who is more than the sum of his or her parts. The Narcissist has the longest path to travel, as he or she must integrate first the multiplicity of characters in her or his shadow side and then begin the process of bringing together the false self with the real.

With so many voices directing our steps, our paths can be confusing and exhausting. The labyrinth is a process for discerning, from a cacophony of noise, the one voice that speaks, the voice that belongs to the one true and united self. This prayer offers us an affirming reminder to keep ourselves unified:

Create in me a divine cooperation
from many selves, one voice
one action.

The dragon of narcissism, however, dissuades us from an integrated state and instead leads us down the path of many selves, dividing its prey into characters such as the Caretaker and the Pretender.

The Caretaker

Leaders and managers who act out the role of the Caretaker do so to create the illusion of their own indispensability. If they can so integrate themselves into an organization that others believe the workplace would be impossible to run without them, they have achieved their objective.

Under the guise of caring, the Caretaker makes as many co-workers as possible dependent upon her or his presence. The Caretaker wins the affection of many unsuspecting victims by assuming a parental role. The Caretaker then treats her or his subordinates as dependent children and instills within them the illusion that they must "hang on" in the parent's absence. This system, with all the characteristics of a dysfunctional family, not only gives a false sense of power to the leader but prevents the empowering of others.

The role of Caretaker is particularly prevalent in religious institutions. In preparation for another book, I have collected church bulletins that reveal the tentativeness and dependence of lay leaders when their clergy is on sabbatical. In public pronouncements, uneasy lay leaders indicate to the congregations that they are "doing their best" and will "hold on" until their leader returns. This dysfunctional attitude is often promoted by the Caretaker, who has set up the system to respond exactly that way. Because the work of religion traditionally has been perceived as a mystical realm only for the professional and the ordained, lay people readily defer to clergy and support such unhealthy systems through a relationship of dependence. True service becomes corrupted by the needy ego of the Caretaker.

This style of management harms not only the people in the Caretaker's orbit, it also diminishes the well-being of the Caretaker. An obvious outcome for someone who must accomplish all things by themselves is workaholism. With an inordinate amount of time devoted to work, the Caretaker loses a balance between private time and work time. Some warning signs of the Caretaker role include:

◎ Inability to delegate responsibly

◎ Disrespect for the experience and skills of others

◎ Portable phones nearby at all times

◎ No time for exercise

◎ Calling in to the office three times daily
when you are on your first vacation in three years

◎ A first vacation in three years

◎ Twelve- to sixteen-hour work days

◎ Few (if any) personal relationships

◎ Weight loss or gain

◎ Increased caffeine intake

◎ Restless sleeping habits

◎ Thinking about work when a family member
or friend is speaking to you

◎ High stress

A CEO who ran a major family business for many years was unwilling to relinquish any of the authority to any of the three family members who were supposedly being groomed for eventual takeover. Although the young vice presidents were given impressive titles and beautiful offices, they had no authority to match the role. The boss made all decisions—down to what kind of copy machines the company should use. His rigid management style resulted in the loss of two of the three VPs who recognized that the scenario was not going to change.

Unfortunately, a father also lost two sons in the process: the boss decided the behavior of his three children (the VPs) was rebellious and insubordinate. To this day, he will not speak to his sons who left the company for a healthier situation.

This obsessively controlling behavior is most common in the circle of leadership and most unfortunate. The need to be always in control not only shuts off the possibility of mentoring new leaders toward a shared vision, but prevents the leader from discovering the magic and power to be discovered within the labyrinth. Any of us can fall prey to this seductive dragon, however. For the leader who is awake, alarms should go off any time we begin to imagine that life will not go on without us. If for even a moment we believe it, we are falling into the illusory trap of the Caretaker.

The Pretender

Like Narcissus, the Pretender loves the look of the exterior. Style reigns over substance, material over meaning. This is a character who thrives on pretense. The Pretender outwardly respects rules and regulations in the secret belief that they do not apply to herself. Her appetites know no limits. She demands immediate gratification, and yet her life is one of unsatisfied desires. Always wanting more, the insatiable cravings become a catalyst for accumulating material things as a way of securing self-worth. Like the dinner host who cooks mountains of food to avoid an assumed public scrutiny if there wasn't enough, the Pretender hoards and accumulates as a way of exhibiting self-importance. A true victim of the mentality of scarcity, the Pretender will extol the virtues of cooperation and teamwork while, in reality, she harbors deep antisocial impulses. Everyone is seen as a rival seeking a portion of her accumulation and ultimately is perceived as a threat to her very existence. Paradoxically, she is fiercely competitive in her demand for approval and acclaim, yet she mistrusts all who might provide that which she seeks.

This type of leader can burn out a staff in a very short time. The combination of very little patience and a constant demand for instant gratification creates unrealistic demands and a frantic work environment. I talked with an employee who picked up the phone every time she saw her manager coming toward her office just to avoid his last-minute agendas, which would often add hours to her work day.

The Pretender has an altered sense of time. He has no appreciation for the past and often disparages it, declaring that whatever existed before is outmoded. Whereas the labyrinth reminds us to look back at where we have been for insights that will pave the path for future action, the Pretender is unable to store experiences that would inform future decisions.

It is not surprising that, enamored by his own reflection, the Pretender has an intense fear of old age. Doing everything possible to maintain the image of youthfulness, the Pretender values physical strength, dexterity, adaptability, and creativity. Because the Pretender devalues older people and believes they have little to contribute, the wisdom of those with more years of experience is seldom appreciated. The result—a terror of becoming old—often leaves the Pretender depressed at turning thirty, in despair at forty, and in full panic at fifty.

Because all his stimulation comes from the external world, the Pretender has a fascination with celebrity status. Company parties celebrating their corporate achievements are notorious for special effects rivaling a Las Vegas floor show. This deep need for exhibition surfaces in individual acts as well.

Overtly or not, the Pretender usually seeks something in return for her services. She gives in order to receive something in return, and there is frequently a high price tag on such an offering. The heroic leader, in contrast, offers her or his service in order to give, to serve, without calculating a return from those who have been served. The Pretender is motivated only by personal gain.

Because of a suspicious and shallow nature, the Pretender enjoys few close friendships. Relationships with others serve only to advance her own personal agenda. Although the Pretender can be the life of the party, her motivation is not from play but to claim the spotlight. Thus, when the crowd has diminished, the Pretender will shrink back behind the protective walls that imprison the once playful child. The Pretenders are tragic characters who truly want to enjoy the inner life of trust, intimacy, and service, yet are stopped by their fear of vulnerability.

We must remember and recognize the dragons of the maze. The dragon of fear prevents us from knowing our deepest self and from taking the risks necessary for any pioneer. The dragon of poor self-concept convinces us that we are unworthy of the journey and the gifts that await the courageous traveler. The dragon of narcissism beckons us to purposes that are self-serving rather than serving others. As authentic leaders, we must confront these dragons with strength and resolve.

The Journey as Natural Evolution

A human family system begins from a union of individuals with a shared vision of a future. Starting in small quarters in simple surroundings, the young family moves forward with a common purpose. When new members of the family arrive, they require special care and attention, and space requirements change. Energetic adolescents need understanding and their "own space" in order to have the freedom to test all of their emerging gifts. As with the family system, if a corporation is to be healthy, it must make room for private space and solitude, tradition and ritual, love and respect.

Companies frequently follow the natural evolutionary stages of birth, infancy, early childhood, adolescence, and maturity, experiencing all the growth pains associated with each passage. Like an adolescent whose body is growing faster than his decision-making capabilities, many firms desire meteoric growth, without a sense of where that growth might lead them or how they can handle it.

Companies riding the crest of new technologies often skyrocket into prominence and then crash with dizzying speed. Firms that endure this rise and fall several times in succession soon have human resource departments that are triage centers whose sole purpose is to infuse just enough energy into exhausted young executives to send them out once again into a frantic marketplace. Said one former head of human resources describing this dynamic, "Because of the extraordinary stress level, we just peel people off the walls and then send them back to the battle front."

Authentic leadership can launch a different system. When a company reaches mature adulthood, its rhythms, balance, and depth are noticeable as its leadership moves with intention and a sense of ease. At a $30-billion company like Hewlett-Packard, for example, one would expect to encounter a frantic work climate; instead one finds the tranquil atmosphere and relaxed pace of a small town.

In the course of my work with the Patnaude Group, I've assisted companies in every stage of the evolutionary process. I have worked with individuals who had an idea and needed to move forward with it immediately in order for it to become a successful reality. As a "work force of one," they began a company with the determination of a baby moving inexorably toward birth. We guide companies in their infancy, helping them create a strategic plan that supports the creative vision that brought them into being.

We encounter many client companies in their adolescent stage experiencing all the struggles of any gawky teenager. Characteristics such as a poor self-concept, high stress, overextended activities, lack of focus, and poor communication skills all require attention if the company is to create a climate for eventual maturity—and success. When such companies do mature, they have a solid system in place that quietly fortifies its members, moving them toward wholeness. Like members of a trusting family who share of themselves because they love one another, the mature company can express the same values. For example, Advanced Micro Devices of Sunnyvale, California, a corporation committed to becoming a learning organization, provides training at every level—from personal development to leadership skills—for its twelve thousand employees. Anyone, whether fabrication worker or executive, can participate regularly in any of the hundreds of training opportunities offered within this learning organization. This is one way for a corporation to say to its employees, "we believe in you and care about you." As a result, the people who work at Advanced Micro Devices feel valued and contribute a higher productivity to the organization.

A Century of Management Change

Over the past century, just as the paradigm for leader
ship is shifting, the practice of management has also
been in the process of development.

In 1911, Frederick Taylor authored *The Principles of
Scientific Management,* a concept some call the most influential
and enduring contribution to Western thought since the
Federalist Papers. According to Taylor, "every single act of the
workman can be reduced to a science." Although Taylor's theo-
ries ushered in efficiency expertise, time and motion studies, and
standardized work procedures, they actually stemmed from the
perception that the worker was lazy and untrustworthy. It was
the management's job to act as a controlling parent, overseeing
the worker's every move, providing the thinking necessary for
any improvements. Management alone was responsible for
ensuring the highest goal, productivity.

In 1933, the original ideas of George Elton Mayo, author of
The Human Problems of an Industrial Civilization, marked a change
in attitude toward labor. Mayo introduced the science of industrial psychology and sociology and initiated the field of human
relations. Mayo believed first that industrial society was diseased
and, second that the manager could serve as a healer. Those employees who were unhappy, he believed, suffered from a mild
form of mental illness; the humanistic manager could serve as a
therapist to the employee patient.

Although Mayo's notions seem off-base or at best, naive,
these ideas paved the way to a more humanistic view of workers'
needs, by encouraging managers to be more effective by learning to understand human behavior. Still the gap between management and employee remained wide. Mayo's ideas still
advocated an elite management and a subservient worker, which
meant that human relations techniques were tools for manipulation, and suspicion and mistrust remained high. In 1945, in *The
Social Problems of an Industrial Civilization* Mayo wrote, "Unlike
the irrational employees he oversees, the administrator of the
future must be able to understand the human social facts...
unfettered by his own emotion or prejudice."

In the 1950s management guru Peter Drucker emerged as the man who promoted management by objectives, writing:

Each manager, from the 'big boss' down to production foreman or the chief clerk, needs clearly spelled out objectives. These objectives should lay out what performance the man's own managerial unit is supposed to produce. They should lay out what contribution he and his unit are expected to make to help other units obtain their objectives. Finally, they should spell out what contribution the manager can expect from other units toward the attainment of his own objectives.

Drucker believed that providing clear objectives would help the worker become more productive. But employee happiness and fulfillment remained irrelevant. "It is not the purpose of business to create happiness," Drucker declared, "but to sell and make shoes." Under Drucker's mentoring, American business continued on its journey toward higher productivity and profit, yet remained deaf to the notion that the employee was the corporation's most valuable resource.

The journey took a major turn in the 1980s when Drucker's position was challenged by high-level corporate consultant Tom Peters, who claimed that the managerial pendulum has swung too far in the direction of Druckerian rationality. "By over-listening to Drucker and his army of simplistic interpreters," he wrote, "we've arrived at a world of management by abstract analysis."

As a human-relations proponent who puts people first, Peters encouraged one of the most important of psychological principles—giving people control over their work. When employees feel as if they have some control over determining the quality of their work environment and the perimeters of their job description, they become more committed to the organization and, usually, more productive. All this is a precursor to discovering a "passion for excellence" (also the title of one of Peters's books), which creates an environment far different from the shop floor of Taylor's era, because:

When you have a true passion for excellence, and when you act on it, you will stand straighter. You will look people in the eye. You will see things happen. You will see heroes created, watch ideas unfold and take shape... You have something to fight about, to care about, to share, scary as it is, with other people. There will be times when you swing from dedicated to obsessed. We don't pretend that it's easy. It takes real courage to step out and stake your claim.

Tom Peters raised one of the most basic concerns in the business arena when he pointed out that individuals necessarily lose some control over their lives when they work within any organization. He helped renew the employee's sense of self, promote the idea that work and passion are related, and forge a path that moves us toward work as art.

Moving from humanism to spirit management, today's managers are more willing to consider how the trust, grace, spirit, and love that reside within them can powerfully and positively affect the work environment. The transformation over the last century is remarkably hopeful, and a clear indicator of the evolution of management's journey.

2 CHOICE

The universe will reward you
for taking risks on its behalf.

SHAKTI GAWAIN

AN ANCIENT JAPANESE PARABLE tells of a samurai master constantly challenged by a student who sought a level of equality with his teacher. The master understood the needs of the young learner and remained patient with him as the student provoked a confrontation at every opportunity. Frustrated by his inability to thwart his teacher, the student conceived a foolproof way to finally conquer his master. Holding a baby bird, he presented his cupped hands to his master and asked: "Is the bird in my hands dead or is it alive?" The master knew if he guessed the bird was dead, the student would open his hands and let the bird fly away. If he said it was alive, a quick squeeze of the student's hands would break the creature's neck, and he would present to the master a dead bird. The master simply looked into the eye of his challenger and said, "It is whatever you choose it to be."

Choice is at the center of our being as it confronts us at every turn of life's labyrinth. We can choose to cut corners or jump over the lines to reach the maze's center. The choice is ours.

The wandering tribes of ancient Israel were no strangers to the circuitous path of the labyrinth. Tradition says that they wandered a desert path for many years before receiving a vision of their destiny. Just before his death, Moses, who had led them out of Egypt and away from the pharaoh's tyranny, stood before them and spoke of the responsibilities inherent in their freedom to choose what lay ahead:

> This day, I have set before you life and death, blessings and curse; therefore choose life so that you and your descendants may live. (Deut. 30:19)

As in the last hopeful words of a dying parent to his children, Moses wanted what was best for his followers who had traveled so far, yet he knew the choice would be theirs to make.

Choice lies at the heart of each of the nine practices of inner management in this book. Living a life of balance, for example, requires the ability to make choices and to say no—and yes. Making use of our expansive imagination involves a conscious decision to not be limited by the confines of a narrow perception but instead to be willing to soar into the uncharted territory of the human mind. Employing intuition means choosing to pay attention to the wisdom within us that speaks without words. Living a life of joy requires a decision to embrace all of life, pain and pleasure, as equal components of wholeness. Authentic power results from making choices that are aligned with compassion—not fear. Business leaders are confronted with an opportunity to choose one path or the other at every hour of every day.

In the first millennium B.C., the ancient mint in Tetradrachm Knossos stamped this famous mythical labyrinth into coins.

Three Elements for Choosing Rightly

> The mind of man is capable of
> anything, because everything is
> in it, all the past as well as all
> the future.
>
> JOSEPH CONRAD

THINKING POSITIVELY

We can encourage positive thinking patterns or cling to the banister of negativity from which we slide downward into the shadow. Negative thinking can create self-fulfilling prophecies. It increases stress, facilitates depression, and chokes creativity. It diminishes our self-esteem as it does our ability to cope effectively with problems and challenges.

Choosing to harbor negative thinking also has disastrous consequences in the work world. I once worked with a friend who repeatedly told himself, unconsciously, that his important projects were doomed to fail. I tried to talk him out of it, but no matter how I assured him, his fear of failure held him intent in the belief that he would not, could not, succeed. Not surprisingly, many of his projects failed, and eventually his company couldn't afford to keep him. He was like the man who sits on a bench in New York's Grand Central Station, throwing sawdust in the air to keep the elephants away. When someone points out to him that there are no elephants in Grand Central Station, he says, "See? It's working!" The elephants for my friend were his images of colossal failure, and eventually he became failure's own best exhibit, never convinced that he had another choice.

Each choice cultivates a habit as well as a direction. My friend who had programmed himself for failure was living in reaction to a cynical interior monologue, a self-punishing habit that destined him for failure. It caused him to focus on the gap between his ambitions and his present conditions, rather than the bridge of possibility that was there for him to cross. By surrendering to negative expectations, he had already fulfilled them.

Negative thinking leads to two especially self-defeating habits. The first is the tendency to base our responses on untested assumptions (such as the possibility of failure) as if they are fact. The other is the habit of having constant second-thoughts about our decisions.

With respect to the first habit, as leaders, it is far more effective to refuse to respond to anything other than objective and demonstrable facts. With respect to the latter, there is no point in speculating about what could have been, when you are confronted with what is. Every choice automatically creates a gain and a loss, a selected path and a road not taken. When we do act, we must have faith that our foundation for leadership is firm enough that we will, in general, choose well.

Mark Twain spoke wisely when he said, "Life does not consist mainly, or even largely, of facts and events. It consists in the main of the storm of thoughts that are forever blowing through one's head." We can't stop our own thought storm, the creative force of our mind. But we can determine the nature of thoughts on which we choose to dwell—to cultivate a direction of thought that is positive and life-enhancing rather than destructive and life-draining.

There are two courses that we can navigate through the storm that rages in our own imagination. The one that will bring us into harbor requires that we leave negative thoughts in our wake, choose to think positively, and act within the realm of self-affirming patterns of thought. Clearly, it is easier to make such a choice in a positive context.

A newly hired scientist, whose first project for her corporate employer resulted in a million-dollar loss, was requested to report to the CEO. The scientist arrived at the executive's office shaking in her shoes. The company president asked her if the facts were straight, and the project had indeed lost all that money. The scientist stammered out a "yes." Rising from his chair, the president thrust out his hand and exclaimed, "Congratulations!" leaving the young woman relieved yet utterly bewildered.

The president continued, "This company has been successful in large part because of our willingness to experiment, take risks, and learn from our failures. If you were to lose another million dollars for the same reason, you'd have to find work elsewhere. We assume you've learned something important from this attempt, and that something great will come of it." That scientist eventually became a valuable contributor to the research organization, producing innovation after innovation.

This example shows how a company can choose to use failures to generate possibilities, rather than as a vehicle for diminishing emerging potential. Corporations who work to discern opportunities rather than obstacles have chosen the higher path of positive thought, which leads not only to unexpected profit but also to new discovery and substantial growth. Such corporate policy begins at the level of individual leadership, at the time and place where the leader makes a choice— not to be a victim of imagined circumstance, but to take responsibility for a well-considered choice and to transform challenging situations to reflect a positive outcome. These are clear and simple acts of will that harness the mind to serve and discover greatness.

ACTING ETHICALLY

The business environment is charged with a host of new issues, involving occupational health, environmental consciousness, affirmative action, international conflicts of interest, and sexual integrity in the workplace, just to name a few. Traditional business ethics are inadequate to answer these moral questions. Furthermore, providing people with a job is no longer adequate justification for a "bottom line" corporate mentality in which profits come before people in every instance. More sophisticated ethical tools are needed for today's business climate.

Accountability

Today, for better or worse, business is accountable at both a societal and personal level. Business decisions affect not only the standard and quality of living for employees, but can help to extend to all people the chance for adequate nutrition, good health, and quality medical care, as well as a life with dignity. These are basic human rights that business leaders can help to ensure, because they, more than any other group, can create solutions to problems within the framework of day-to-day realities.

Peter Drucker, one of the architects of modern management, has said that "efficiency is doing the thing right, while effectiveness is doing the right thing." When business leaders ask themselves the question "What is the right way?," they frequently mean what is politically expedient or good for profits in the short run. Here's an example of what happens when management instead begins to explore what is good for the company and humanity over the long term.

Wetherill Associates, Inc., an auto-electric parts distributor based in Royersford Pennsylvania. According to E. Marie Bothe, president of WAI, the company was incorporated in 1978 with an express purpose of advancing a moral concept—to translate right actions into right results in accord with a behavioral law of nature discovered by Richard Wetherill. The founders were members of Wetherill's study group and they sought to demonstrate the validity of the behavioral law through the sharing of an economic opportunity, requiring honesty, integrity, and accountability within its infrastructure and toward customers and suppliers. The company has proved to be a long-lived, spectacular experiment. In 1991, sales reached $70 million, a figure that Wetherill officials point to as a natural outcome of their support for the Right-Action-Ethic™. 1995 was another record year with sales exceeding $131 million. By enforcing a no-gifts-accepted policy, refusing to give kickbacks, and dealing with customers honestly, WAI has raised the quality performance of an industry not previously known for high ethical standards.

> Whatever one's philosophical or even
> theological position, a society is not
> the temple of value, devoted to its
> idols that figure in front of its monu-
> ments, or to its constitutional scrolls.
> The value of a society is the value it
> places on man's relation to man.
>
> MAURICE MERLAU-PONTY

As we have discussed, business today has the financial network and technological capabilities to shape the destiny of humanity. Such a responsibility requires leaders who will address
needs effectively and a business ethic based on the spiritual
value of human dignity. Corporate culture must seek not only
the optimum relationship among risk, reward, and profit, it
must foster initiative, sharing, and community.

Doing what is right profits all our lives and plows a wider
strip of ground than the narrow focus of the traditional corporate bottom line. I believe that businesses that choose to act
ethically are ultimately more profitable than those obsessed
with the net. Doing good for its own sake requires a shift in the
managerial paradigm. The decision-making authority invested
in management results in an ethical conflict between the manager and employee when the employee is not consulted about
important company decisions. Management must explore new
ways of sharing that authority in order to establish a more com-
prehensive ethic for in-company culture.

The policy of Missouri's Springfield Remanufacturing
Company—with a workforce of 800 and 1995 earnings of over
$100 million—is to treat employees "as if they own the place."
Hence, production workers receive exactly the same information in their weekly meetings about every penny earned and
spent as the board of directors, and participate in making corporate decisions right along with management. Springfield's
open book management has been called a turnaround strategy
for American capitalism, and such large corporations as Xerox
and Clorox send teams of executives to The Great Game of
Business seminars to learn from the Springfield model.

The effect of corporate decisions is not isolated within the
organization, but touches human society as a whole. Every
individual who thinks and acts ethically contributes to a

universal moral climate. Our every action makes a difference, just as every thought registers within the energy pool of the cosmos. Ethical thinking contributes toward a positive environment of imagination and hope.

TELLING THE TRUTH

"Character," Aristotle wrote, "is a matter of habit." We develop a truthful character simply by choosing to tell the truth. The opposite is also true. As M. Scott Peck writes in *People of the Lie*, the more lies we tell, the closer we move toward embodying our lies. Each lie becomes the delight of the dragon of fear who feasts on each morsel in anticipation of the entrée of our whole being.

Sometimes in the midst of often frantic and complex professional decisions, it is difficult to distinguish between solid facts and the apparent realities created by a high-pressure environment. Here, the body itself is one of our greatest aids. The body is a sensor of what is true and what is not. Because we can easily deceive ourselves in our minds, the body becomes the filter for discerning the truth. If, for example, I begin saying something that I know is not grounded in fact, my throat clogs up, and I find it necessary to clear my throat repeatedly. Questioned by an audience, speakers offering answers that are half-lies awkwardly give themselves away. Eyes roll, hands fidget, voices quiver, and feet pace. The body rebels when the brain tries to drag it into doing something without the body's permission. This is a basic lesson that a wise and seasoned poker player learns early.

Truth is the basic currency of human social relations. It is what stabilizes society, and what allows for its existence. Consider this: if lying were the standard behavior in a society, all knowledge would have to be self-acquired. No one could trust what was learned from another. Economics as we know it could not function: imagine if you couldn't trust your supplier's delivery promise, or your floor manager's assurance that your product would be ready for shipment within the week. Truthfulness is the lifeblood of the corporation; it forms the final cornerstone—alongside thinking positively and acting ethically—in choosing the right path.

Dictator to Pragmatist:
A Case History of Robert Lorenzini

BY ROBIN NEFF

Choice is perhaps the foremost theme in Bob Lorenzini's
personal pathway to leadership. Founder and former
owner of the Siltec Corporation, Bob began this silicon
manufacturing company in 1969 so that he could run a
business "his way." After an unsatisfying business partnership in
Elmat Corporation, Bob's new venture meant that he would be
the general at the front lines, preparing new troops for a battlefield he knew well: Silicon Valley. By 1984 Siltec employed more
than 500 people, and brought in over $500 million in sales. The
company ran like a highly skilled army; everyone knew the drills,
everyone knew their specific function. "And all the time I was in
the command station," Bob smiles wryly. There's pride in his
voice, and also chagrin. He remembers the unending pressure
and the loneliness of his post. It had all come down to him—
every last decision from key financial matters to where to buy
postage stamps. Bob believed that because he was the only one
aware of every crucial detail, he alone could be trusted to make
decisions for his company. Team work? Bob almost laughed at
the notion.

Bob had been so busy with short-range operations of silicon
wafer manufacturing that he hadn't paid attention to the steady
influx of large chemical manufacturing companies into the
Silicon Valley. So when Eurosil, a leading European chemical
producer, approached him with a $45-million offer for Siltec,
his response ran the gamut from surprise to flattered to cocky.
He reasoned that if Eurosil was willing to pay that much, surely
someone else would offer a lot more months down the road.
All he had to do was to keep the business under control.

In Bob's mind, the influx of international companies like
Bynimit Nobel, Osaka Titanium, Wacker Chemicals, and Shih Etsu
Hondotai had no significant ramifications. He had lead his army
to victory so far and there was no reason to believe that he
wouldn't be able to do so in the future.

Looking back, Bob cringes as he remembers where his leadership strategy led Siltec. Because he had insisted on keeping
such strong control, especially financially, his balance sheet could

not begin to compete with the capital power of the larger corporations. They could afford to incur debt without punishment, whereas Siltec could not. By the end of 1986 Bob had been forced to cut 25 percent of his work force and drastically cut all expenditures. An expansion project already under way in Oregon was abandoned. Clearly, Bob could no longer keep one step ahead of his competition by sheer willpower, scrupulous attention to detail, and unyielding control. When he finally sold Siltec in late 1986, the company was a weaker version of itself, a fact reflected in the $33-million selling price.

Bob's entrance into the maze required letting go of the past. He reflected on the shortcomings of his narrow, controlling leadership style and concluded it could no longer work. He needed to develop a new openness to ideas and information, to increase his collaborative efforts with other experts. He gradually realized that there were other people who knew as much about running a business as he did.

When Bob reached the maze's center, he sought inspiration about what business he should pursue. He had essentially fallen into silicon wafer manufacturing, but saw no reason to continue with it now. As if someone had removed a set of blinders, Bob became aware of the many aspects of life he had chosen to ignore for the past eighteen years.

His daughter was beginning college just as his son was graduating. Bob had been so obsessed with running a successful business that he had missed out on much of their childhood. He had tried to control everything and everybody in the same style in which he'd run his company. The rewards had been as narrow as his focus. During the course of two decades Bob had gained financial success and little else.

As a participant in the EAGLES seminars, traveling the path of the maze, Bob recognized his need to release some of his control and to allow his life to open up. And without being fully conscious of it, this awareness changed him. Standing smack in the center of the maze, Bob knew that the only pathway lay ahead, a circuitous route full of unknowns and surprises.

The year following Bob's newfound awareness of what he wanted from life was spent relearning how to be an entrepreneur. But this time it wasn't a solo effort. Bob essentially went back to the beginning, capitalizing on his relationship with Stanford professors. What new research was going on? How could it be turned into a business? Who were the experts in the field? These questions were all geared toward gathering information and putting together a team of people whose collaborative efforts would be greater than the product of each laboring alone. The business was secondary. Setting up a leadership culture combining experience, imagination, trust, and fun was primary. With that in place Bob could shed the role of commander-in-chief and take on a role of mediator—a coordinator of great talent and potential.

In 1988 his vision came to fruition. Through the recommendation of the Electric Power Resource Institute (EPRI), Bob met with some scientists at Stanford, Professor Dick Swanson and Research Engineer Dick Crane, to discuss the development of a new solar cell which they believed to be the marketable answer to the solar power dilemma. The idea appealed to Bob because it was an opportunity to help create a product with positive environmental impact. After looking into the feasibility of the product and testing the venture capital market for interest, Bob and his team officially launched the manufacturing of solar power cells. SunPower Corporation was born. The early days were heady, full of excitement and anticipation. SunPower's leaders would meet in Dick Swanson's office; ideas flew around like flies. The energy level was immeasurable. Gone was the lonely pressure Bob felt at Siltec. The support of his colleagues afforded him the luxury of exploring ideas broader than his previously limited focus would allow, and it paid off. In 1993, SunPower's cells were used in Honda's solar-powered race car, which not only won, but set a world record at the Australian race from Darwin to Adelaide.

Bob Lorenzini emerged from the maze to look back at where his path had led him. "The leader I was in the 1970s and early 1980s would have scoffed at terms like "intuition" and "compassion" in the context of business. Without the experience, [of selling Siltec for less money than first offered] I would never have been open to the concept of EAGLES. What I found in my year attending seminars was an affirmation of my instincts toward business and personal practices. I learned that trust, balance, imagination, and compassion were not only nice words, but powerful business tools. The experience of sharing this with other business leaders was invaluable. To this day we [the people in Bob's EAGLES group] maintain strong connections that serve us personally and professionally."

3 BALANCE

The spirit is enormously talented
at providing you with people and
circumstances to steadily heal
your wounds, meet your needs,
and bring you into balance.

MARY HAYES-GRIECO

AN ASTUTE OBSERVER of the business world referred to today's business climate as "permanent white water." Indeed, barreling down a thundering river in a small craft is an apt metaphor for today's business climate. How do people survive, much less flourish, in such an unpredictable environment? Some advisors insist that we need to learn how to thrive on chaos. I disagree.

Thriving on Balance

The first step, I believe, is the discovery that we thrive on balance—that innate stability known to the ancients. It stems from attention to the relationship of body, mind, and spirit as we live and work in the world. From there, we can set a course wherein our work becomes not merely a means for survival, but something that helps us to express and practice our God-given talents and abilities.

It's simply a fact of business life that competition from foreign markets rocks and pulls at many companies until they threaten to capsize or run aground. Technology causes product lines to become obsolete almost instantly.

On a plane recently, a well-groomed high-tech executive waxed enthusiastic about his company's "flash card"—a computer disk the size of a credit card that could contain 60 million bytes of information and sold for about $400. It used RISC-chip technological principles that virtually make it possible to carry a workstation in your wallet. It sounded impressive to me until I saw an article in the paper a few days later: it said that another device employing the same technology could hold 200 million bytes, would plug not only into a computer, but also a telephone, and would sell for about $79. My planemate's device was less than two weeks old, and already it was obsolete. It's safe to say that a whole marketing strategy had just gone out the window and that some haggard R&D department would take a blow to the solar plexus and have to find the strength to rebound.

To roll with the kind of punches one must absorb in today's business world takes an extraordinary sense of balance. To use an earthquake metaphor, how do we achieve a capacity to remain upright when the whole world is shaking? How can we learn to survive intact, even when risk and uncertainty loom around every corner?

Sources of Balance

The best answer is to discover sources—and resources—for maintaining our balance. Yet in many corporations, even such basic improvements as striking a realistic balance between expectations and working conditions may not be a strong priority. Managers need to notice not only employee attendance, but also the quality of the work environment: light sources in the office, food selection in the cafeterias, ergonomics of desk chairs.

Although awareness about workstation ergonomics is now common and there is a growing concern for the physical well-being of the worker, too many workplaces still resemble dark, uncomfortable caves. The absence of light, color, and foliage creates a sterile environment that inhibits creativity, and often, production.

Ironically, most of us instinctively head for the outdoors

when we vacation, as a way of renewing our inner balance, frequently diminished at work. When we learn to incorporate more aspects of the natural environment into our work environment, we unify the worlds of spirit and business.

Balance with Passion and Purpose

Thanks to creative and compassionate entrepreneurs, concern for balance is growing as a corporate objective. As we learn more about the role that balance plays in the practice of inner management, we emerge with more than a mere checklist of creature comforts under the headings of body, mind, spirit. What emerges is a pervasive awareness, a capacity to translate the search for harmony into the very structure and philosophy of the corporation, there to establish a dynamic relationship—originating within the company and moving outward into the world.

THE BODY SHOP

This trend in business leadership is exemplified by Anita Roddick, who heads the immensely successful international Body Shop chain. At present the company counts some 700 stores and franchise outlets in thirty-nine countries. Though Roddick's company is now valued at $1.2 billion, it began sixteen years ago with a small line of fifteen products and a modest hope to make ends meet after an investment of about $300 a month. Roddick has gathered beauty product ideas from a variety of cultures worldwide. Her company's remarkable success has been fueled by a desire to change the world through the universal medium of trade. Roddick supplies high-quality cosmetics to a growing number of people worldwide, while maintaining standards about the ecological impact her products can have. For example, the Body Shop was one of the first retailers to allow customers to bring back containers for refilling. A more complex example of Roddick's philosophy lies in her efforts to make sure that the harvesting of the ingredients in her products benefits the people and the land where they are grown; when she discovered recently that an ingredient in a product was not organic as the manufacturer claimed, she discontinued the product rather than allow her customers to buy a product that wasn't earth smart.

Supplying customers with aesthetically pleasing cosmetics while considering the impact of those cosmetics on our planet is Roddick's passion and purpose.

TOM'S OF MAINE

Another company that devotes an extraordinary amount of attention to balance is Tom's of Maine, Incorporated, producer of natural personal hygiene products. Headed by CEO Tom Chappell, the firm's sales revenues for 1992 alone totaled over $17 million. Yet Chappell speaks about his company's purpose in language that reveals not only a concern for profit, but a respect for values. "Business," he says, "is about both the world of incentives and the world of love. When you act out of love and concern for your customers and the people who work for you, you get the best of everything."

Chappell studied for four years at Harvard Divinity School, where he became fascinated by the implications of theology for business. He asked Richard R. Niebuhr, a professor from Harvard to lead a management retreat that explored Immanuel Kant's connection between freedom and responsibility, and invited Arthur Dyck, a professor of ethics, to help draft a company mission statement based on this blueprint. He freely admits that he manages the business "upside down."

"I fell into the trap that a lot of business people do," he says. "I started working for the numbers. The company was producing good results, but I asked myself, 'what is the kick here?'" Returning to his original desire to blend spirit and business, Tom changed directions. Today, more than 10 percent of Tom's pre-tax profit is donated to address problems of the environment and human need. "It is our responsibility," Chappell comments, "to hold the environment in our consideration as much as the consumer and the profits of the company. These things have to be equally balanced."

The balance that Tom Chappell and Anita Roddick both cultivate telegraphs itself to the work environment and inspires confidence. If a leader is demonstrably "in synch," the company as a whole has access to unique energy and vision. Project teams are better able to meet any challenge enthusiastically and creatively because balance has enabled the leader calmly to embrace and communicate her or his own intuition and imagination. The result is that confident vision and effective collaboration can be seen throughout the company.

Spirit in Business

In our traditional conception, spirit and business lie on oppo-site ends of the spectrum. Yet ancient wisdom suggests that the desired path inevitably lies between extremes. The Tao-te Ching, that often enigmatic collection of the sayings of the Chinese sage Lao-tzu, tells us:

The Divine Way is like the drawing of a bow; it brings down the high and exalts the low... It is the way of heaven to diminish abundance, and supplement deficiency. (Chapter 77)

This is not to say that balance comes from bland compro-mise or by sitting on the fence. Instead of merely staking out a spot in the middle, balance is found at an equidistant center, like the serene eye of a storm wherein all the forces pull sym-metrically. Achieving an internal environment of balance in the executive's world of constant change and chaos is a great chal-lenge and an important necessity. This chapter looks at ways to achieve such internal balance and to extend that personal inte-gration toward concern for our work environment. It catalogs some benefits of creating a work climate where, after years of service, employees depart healthier and wiser.

Harmony in the Workplace

The creation of a workplace that promotes harmony and bal-ance calls to mind common ground shared by business and culture. Work spaces that sacrifice form to function by failing to provide art, ornament, and design to please the senses and encourage reflection may be efficient places, but they ignore physical, mental, and spiritual well-being.

BALANCE THROUGH ART

Throughout human history, art has always helped satisfy our yearning for balance. Many images found within the world's fine artworks can serve us well as guides in the pursuit of bal-ance. The symmetry and muscular confidence evinced by the famous Discus Thrower, originally cast in bronze by a Greek sculptor about 450 B.C. and copied by virtually every civiliza-tion since Roman times, reveals a millennia-old admiration for balance as expressed in athletics. Much more recently, photographer Ansel Adams captured three women dancing with precarious grace at the edge of Yosemite's Inspiration Point, aided only by the balancing weight of a fragile umbrella.

GLOBAL BALANCE

Balance is much more than a trick to keep on your feet in perilous times. I believe it is the secret of the universe. It is an observable fact that imbalance only begets further imbalance. On a planetary level, that observation is alarming. Snowless winters, intense flooding, and prolonged droughts are indicators that this beautiful, living organism (of which we are a part) is not at all well. Global industrialism, motivated solely by the bottom line, is largely responsible. This decade may be the last opportunity to turn the tide against environmental degradation and to restore the ecology of the natural order. Today's leaders must take the reins.

When we permit imbalance to overcome the workplace, we become trapped in the shopworn paradigm of power and profit, rather than a true empowerment built upon respect, with decisions that reflect group consensus rather than top-down mandates. We need employees and executives who can contribute to the emergence of a more effective, human-centered business model.

A NEW LANGUAGE

A new language is forming to describe the workings of such new business communities achieving balance within themselves, for the marketplace, and in the world.

Society itself stands on the threshold of an enormous transformation, a change so momentous that the word sometimes used to describe it by ancient Greek theologians is the term *metanoia*. Its most basic meaning is "a turning around, a conscious change of direction." Within the business community, new concepts such as the "stakeholder" combine the concept of "employees," "stockholders," "clients," "customers," and "management," underscoring that each of these people now have a clear interest in the enterprise that transcends and moves beyond profit alone. "Stakeholder" is an inclusive term connoting participation in decisions, a common sense of ownership, and responsibility. In a related vein, we hear reference to some corporations as being "value-led," as opposed to profit-driven, and to measuring success at least in part as a function of clear values, consistently expressed.

A Corporation in Balance

The Radian Corporation of Austin, Texas, employs some 2,100 people, half of whom are scientists and engineers producing innovative technological solutions for global environmental problems—from providing environmental management services to tracking hazardous chemical gases. Since 1969, Radian has benefited from leadership that inspires balance. Radian sees itself as a company on a quest, but, as Neal Kocurek, Senior Vice President of the Technical Staff, likes to say, the company does not journey alone, but instead invites both clients and employees to join in as fellow travelers.

Radian's goal has been to provide a quality working environment for employees, while maintaining a technological standard that can meet the public's critical need and improve and preserve the environment. To fulfill these objectives, Radian relies on a triad of concerns that balance and guide its corporate decisions. Employees are expected to consider how any decision will affect the client, the shareholder, and all employees. The respect that Radian cultivates for these three groups, Neal Kocurek says, means that "integrity is Radian's number-one corporate value."

Don Carlton, President and CEO of Radian, has been with the company since its founding. A tall, trim man of fifty-seven, Carlton strikes the outsider's imagination as the ideal Texas gentleman. He is both at ease and playful—a manner befitting an executive who loves what he does, and who is also a devoted father and grandfather. Carlton is very much aware of the value of human connection and communication. One small incident sums up his character for me: When we first spoke about the quality of balance in professional life, it was plain he'd thought about it before. He launched into an answer, then stopped himself and smiled, saying in a deep and gracious drawl, "But I'm just rambling. How can I respond best to you?"

It's that conscious desire to encourage participation that has marked Carlton's approach to corporate growth at Radian. "Whoever sits at the top of the heap is pretty important," he says, "but all those others are pretty important, too. As we've gotten larger over the years, through difficult as well as good times, we've attempted to stay together, even though we employ people of radically different personalities who may have a hard time staying at the table."

Basic to maintaining a fulfilling work environment is the concept that it's frustration that gets to people, not hard work. "We preach that at Radian," Don points out, "but we practice it, too. Whenever possible, we ask people to do for the company what they do best, and not try to put the square peg in the round hole." Employees respond to being viewed as important individuals: annual turnover at Radian averages only about 5 percent.

Though Radian now boasts twenty-five offices throughout the United States, with eleven international offices and affiliates, the corporation started with eleven employees in 1969. It began its organization chart with four vice presidents who reported to Carlton, which meant only a few people reported to each VP. That configuration appeared to work well for about four years, by which time Radian had grown to about one hundred employees. In the beginning, the company was housed in a space of about 4400 square feet, about the same floor space as a large house. Don could stand at his office door, raise his voice, and everybody could hear him, "That," he reflects, "was perfect communication!" With rapid growth, that intimate geography disappeared—now some employees were working in trailers behind the main building, while others worked down the street. Communication didn't happen automatically, and further expansion has compounded that problem.

Like horses on a cattle drive—to use Texas imagery—strings of people had become attached to those original vice presidents, and they also tended to reflect the personal characteristics of the leading horse at the head of the string. A super-scientist would tend to hire other super-scientists, a top salesperson would attract people who could sell but not necessarily bring a project to completion. There was diversity, but it was not valued or distributed to properly serve the company's mission.

In 1973, Radian reorganized its corporate structures from its linear model to that of a "matrix." It formed teams with people of diverse preferences and abilities, so that sales, science, and project management would receive balanced attention in every project. Don considers this a watershed decision for Radian.

"The most important thing we could do from a management standpoint," he told me, "was to focus on the capabilities of our people and try to array those against the task that needed to be done."

This meant not only identifying particular gifts but honoring them. It made a difference in employee evaluations. Don remembered when Jim Dickerman, a manager who excelled in sales, was asked to evaluate the strengths and weaknesses of his staff. Under the old system, a sales manager might well have measured a subordinate's contributions against his own sales-driven standards. Since the Radian matrix, built on diversity of personality, responses were more balanced and accurate, and the project stood to benefit. At one point Jim gave the example of a woman on his team who disliked cold calls, and who didn't do well in personally building client relationships. "But she writes the best proposals I've ever seen," he said, 'They are clear, lucid, right to the point. That really sells the company to the client." The obvious conclusion was to have her write the team's proposals, and thus permit her work (rather than the strength of her personality) to help the project. In order to uncover that conclusion, team leaders need to be alert to the need for a balance of attributes, structuring teams in such a way that individual strengths complement one another, and weaknesses become less and less of a problem.

Another example of that principle at work is a particular vice president who, in Don's words, "does nothing but be a smart guy." Consumer analysis consistently reveals that Radian gets a lot of business as a direct consequence of his scientific brilliance, but no one reports to him because responsibility for subordinates or for the nuts and bolts of "P & L" would make him less effective. Other technical people are on the same track, with all appropriate perks, because, as Don has said, "You don't have to sell a bunch of stuff or have a lot of people sending you reports to have a career at Radian."

A second element basic to Radian's corporate balance lies in the fact that it's not the individual who gets the credit or corporate leverage. Those who understand success in terms of "power and perks" need to retrack their thinking if they come to work at Radian. Surroundings are comfortable, and people are treated with respect, but names on parking slots, important-sounding titles, substantial office suites, and first-class plane flights are not part of the executive's package. Furthermore, recognition is a team concept. "We don't pay commissions," Don says. "If someone's work wins a contract, then we all have won a contract. At our annual achievement award dinner, outstanding employees, first nominated by their peers and then selected by the vice presidents, receive a $1000 cash award and a plaque. We have an award category for people who simply have been solid performers for a long time, even if they've never accomplished a breakthrough or done something extraordinary. I think people should be rewarded for the unspectacular but solid performance. Not everybody gets a chance to be there when the bomb goes off!"

A third factor in providing a climate to do a job well is to recognize that family support—however an individual might define "family"—is crucial in lessening frustration and disharmony. "Whenever we have any corporate function," Don explains, "it's also a family function, whether it's our annual award banquet, the Christmas party, or the company picnic. An employee's performance is strongly influenced by the support they receive from home. We always try to recognize that support."

The Radian corporate matrix features a balance among power, the value of people and community. Not only does Radian acknowledge the role of family as a motivating factor for employees, but it sets its own company structure within a larger context as well. The "Radian triad" has three points that stabilize its work—customer, shareholder, and employee. A fair return to the shareholder and employee satisfaction both emanate from the response of the customer. Contracts reap profits, and profits mean dividends, but the good opinion of the client is the point that stands at the center of that triad. Don Carlton states his conviction this way: "Some people respond to a kick in the tail, others to a pat on the back. A pat on the back from a client is the best it gets. If we serve our clients well, all the other good things will follow."

There is a fourth point which, although not a formal part of Radian's corporate geometry, is an important factor for a company that combats pollution and tackles environmental challenges and whose employees have a strong sense that what they do contributes to the healing of the earth. To the customer/shareholder/employee structure of consideration might be added society, as Radian seeks, in serving its customers, to give back to the environment that supports them all, customer and company alike.

"There's no doubt," says Don, "that serving society motivates our people. We are a business, not a charitable organization. There are things you have to do to be successful, but additionally, we have the feeling that what we are doing is important for the world's future.

Rather than equate success with the acquisition of power or profit, or see effectiveness as a measure of how one manages others, Radian offers the model of a balanced work environment where people can grow and work out their individual purpose, to benefit the client, the company, and themselves while making the world a better place in which to live.

Staying in Balance

Striving for balance is the first step to effective management, both inside and out. You can't do anything well without it. Balance is crucial to becoming fully human, and thus is also essential to feeling fully alive in the workplace. Becoming balanced is one thing; staying in balance is equally essential. The cultivation of balance is a learning process that draws us into situations that test our ability to keep on our feet. To embark on this kind of journey is often the consequence of a hard, perhaps inevitable turn in one's professional road. Often people who rest within corporations do not want to surrender the perquisites that keep them dependent on a dysfunctional or otherwise unbalanced style of management, much less of living. Yet the greater challenge is to break free of the things that bind us there, and remain within the structure, changed yet strengthened.

MAINTAINING BALANCE IN LIFE AND WORK

Proclaiming the role of business in social transformation in their book *Creative Work*, William Harman and John Hormann wrote, "Inherent in [the] picture of a society transforming itself are severe challenges to the individual; since we all face them, we can draw strength from one another."

In keeping with this idea, this chapter contains some hands-on suggestions for achieving balance in one's life and work. You are invited to examine them and make them a part of your life of leadership.

A PYRAMID OF BALANCE

A model based on a triad of elements, issues, or options is a useful way to achieve balance. While two elements create a bi-polar way of thought with the balance point along a linear path, three areas of focus set up a pyramid of balance.

The Hebrew prophet Micah said that the formula for good-ness rests on three practices—doing justice, loving kindness, and walking humbly with God. Sixteen centuries ago, in an-other triad model, St. Augustine wrote that God's three princi-pal gifts to humankind—and the foundation for our very nature—are memory, reason, and skill. Likewise, this book is constructed around three primary movements, a way of being, of knowing, and of action. Focusing too much on one element creates imbalance.

Steps Toward Balance

To balance issues of my life, I determine the key elements of any concern and try to live somewhere near the center of my triangle. I balance my time between learning, earning, and serving. I encourage a sense of well-being by balancing atten-tion toward mind, body, and spirit. And I balance my life pur-pose by attending to the essential elements I learned some years ago:

⑨ Sit quietly
⑨ Love my family
⑨ Do what needs to be done

SIT QUIETLY

Theologian Henri Nouwen once described the spiritual journey as one from absurdity (from the Latin *ab* + *surdus*, deaf) to obe-dience (from the Latin *ob* + *audiens*, listening with intention). Like the bemused Midwestern farmer in the movie *Field of Dreams* who plows his cornfield under to build a baseball field in response to insistent inner voices, we too must be ready to hear improbable wisdom when we grow attentive to what is uttered from the silence within us.

A person who feels out of balance may simply not be paying sufficient attention to the restorative power of silence. The tendency for otherwise healthy people to take so-called "mental health days" is often simply a bid to recover some quiet time. Unfortunately, we fill that time with activity—shopping, entertainment, running family errands, even seeking another job. When do we take the time to just sit, tune out the noise, and in the quiet, to listen?

In the workplace, quiet is often in short supply. Usually noise resounds at several levels. In meetings, when someone is speaking, colleagues are most often rehearsing their own answers, practicing their own voice so they will appear insightful, rather than really listening to what the presenter is saying. Even when only one voice is audible, the conference room is filled with mental babble. Giving one's self over to the calming, centering of martial arts exercises or the privacy of a journal, or the measured steps of a solitary walk in the woods, are to my mind a vital part of any planning process. These silent spaces not only restore balance, but provide stimulus for a fresh set of truly new ideas.

> I have a very busy and full life
> and occasionally am asked, 'Scotty,
> how can you do all that you do?'
> The most telling reply I can give
> is: 'Because I spend two hours a
> day doing nothing.' Ironically, the
> questioner usually responds by
> saying he's too busy to do that.
>
> M. SCOTT PECK

The Balance Provided by a Quiet Retreat

Sometimes a retreat is necessary in order to maintain true silence. Japanese business executives build harmony into their professional lives by retreating to tranquil spaces where they can recover a sense of balance and reflective stability. Executives here also need such places, whether they're in one's own

office or in a place more traditionally associated with balance
and peace of mind—a church, a park, a corner of the back
yard at home.

LOVE YOUR FAMILY

The second imperative for my life—loving my family—has a
broader meaning for me than just being nice to relatives. In the
Middle Ages, "family" meant everyone who was part of the
household—it included not only spouse, children, parents, but
also those who worked to preserve the integrity of the household and those whose friendship kept them connected to the
family's best interests. "Family" had a connotation that was
more like the modern use of "community," and that's how I understand that second imperative. It also requires that I be selective in choosing and building family relationships, because
they signify a deep, unconditional commitment that demands
my loyalty, my time, and my support.

Taking care to cultivate meaningful relationships in one's
personal life has a strong parallel for business connections,
which are no longer to be taken lightly. The objective of many
companies in the past has been to make a single sale or secure
a one-time contract of service. More often today, companies try
to secure a client's business for an entire generation or longer.
This was once the case in more stable communities of a century or more ago, where long-standing connections, built on
trust and customer loyalty, were deeply valued. It's more difficult to achieve in our volatile society but perhaps more necessary today than ever before.

DO WHAT NEEDS TO BE DONE

It's exhausting and time-consuming to work with co-workers
who need constant overseeing and direction simply because
they are not able to see what needs to be done. Thomas Edison
used to guard against this with an unusual interview technique.
He would drop a large paper wad on the floor of his office between the door and his desk. Interviewees who did not stop to
pick up the paper were off to an irrevocably bad start with

Edison: according to him, they'd revealed themselves to be people who could not see something that needed to be done.

Edison's style may have been eccentric, but he had a point. Doing what needs to be done is the third, and certainly from a contemporary corporate standpoint, a most important element for a life plan. Today's emerging model for leadership is collaborative, and its success relies in large part on cooperation and personal initiative.

The key to mediocrity is doing only what is necessary. Coloring strictly within the lines of one's job description spells doom for a corporation. Doing what needs to be done, even when it's unexpected, is more than a personal challenge—it's a necessity for corporate success.

Within this new world of work, it's axiomatic that if we don't love what we do, we should shift our sights to do what we love. What this means is that the first point of the triangle for fulfillment in one's work is the discovery of one's passion, so often squelched by an inordinate concern for planning and predictable order.

In the stillness of your sacred space, allow your imagination free play around a desired goal, and draw out from your reflection the three most important elements to consider for achieving that goal. Prepare to be surprised—creativity dwells in the realm of the unexpected. Don't be too anxious to supply answers; allow space for important questions to be asked. Set the triangle of what you'll do in balance with how you serve and who you love. By maintaining this deep sense of balance in the face of life's uncertainties, you are preparing ground for a well-founded and rewarding practice of the art of inner management.

THE CENTER OF THE MAZE

A Way of Knowing

PURPOSE:

To reflect in a place of sacred illumination
so that imagination and intuition can guide us.
From this place the leader receives components of
the vision that will allow her or him to move toward action.

DISCIPLINE FOR MASTERY:

Release

PRACTICES OF
INNER MANAGEMENT:

• Imagination • Intuition
• Joy

What lies behind us and what lies before us are tiny matters compared to what lies within.

RALPH WALDO EMERSON

Having journeyed the precarious road of a way of being, we arrive at the place of center, a treasure room for knowing the unknowable. It is here in the realm of imagination, intuition, and joy that the traveler is gifted with inspiration, confirmation, and the celebration of a solution or vision that will be employed in the final trilogy, a way of action. We can stay here as long as we choose to ponder the wisdom and vision that occurs in union with the sacred.

One of the most popular spiritual works of the middle ages was a piece of mystical reflection entitled *The Cloud of Unknowing*. Its anonymous author suggested that the way to prepare the mind to receive the Divine was to clear it of all preexisting knowledge and to create a tabula rasa, or blank slate, on which true consciousness might find a resting place.

Knowledge can be defined in many different ways. Scientists rely on knowledge that is observable. The police act on evidence that is verifiable. Clergy make claims based on faith. Stockbrokers trade on trends that they believe are predictable. Visionary leadership explores knowledge simply because it is imaginable, yet unrealized. To express such vision, leaders need tools that will link creativity with the world.

Three invaluable tools for the visionary leader are imagination, intuition, and joy, together forming a triad that illuminates a way of knowing. The realm of the imagination is where our most creative visions and thoughts arise, unrestricted by conventional assumptions of what is logical or possible. We are all aware of the existence of our imagination but we need to nurture it and reestablish its value. Through intuition, which allows our restricted consciousness to reconnect with the visionary dimension that fires imagination, we can reach joy. Joy is the eternal playful spirit every child knows, that is often repressed by the weight of too much knowledge or structure and is always resurrected by love for life. Joyful people are enthusiastic people, moved by a zest for living, borne on the wings of imagination, empowered by a strong gift of intuition.

What if we were to forsake a plodding and exclusive reliance on what we can prove and embrace instead a different way of knowing suggested by imagination, sustained by intuition, and expressed through joy? Those who have dared to do so have often drawn closer to the original, creative spirit that dwells within, and discovered new and exciting ways to live and to work.

The place of center will reveal that it is sometimes necessary to throw out all preconceptions and be open to a process that welcomes creative change. Children do this every time they knock down the blocks of a tower for the pure pleasure of seeing it fall. Artists and scientists also follow this process, which often brings them to the place where they feel the deepest inspiration. When Albert Einstein posited his Theory of Relativity, for example, he first had to let go of every principle he'd learned. Claude Monet's impressionism broke new ground redefining the conventions of visual art. Indeed, the painter once said that he wished he had been born blind and later been given sight, so that he would never have been exposed to the conditioned responses to light and color and form, and been free to see the world with entirely new eyes.

As we mature, we often lose the ability to act spontaneously. Play can become as structured and scheduled as a staff meeting or the annual Christmas party. When play lacks spontaneity, we lose our creativity.

The essential connection between doing and being is forged by a sense of joy. We can never link who we are with what we do until we do what we love. What we love is that which makes our heart sing. When work is merely a necessity, a dry and lifeless exercise in rote production, we will step back from it when we want to feel most fully alive and dissociate work from our sense of self. When we take the risk to do what we love, work becomes art, a vital expression of self-identity.

4 IMAGINATION

> I am certain of nothing but the
> holiness of the heart's affections
> and the truth of imagination.
>
> JOHN KEATS

IN AN ERA OF SUCH RAPID CHANGE, one of the primary challenges to business is to remain creative. Today, "working smarter" means discovering new ways to work. Creating more productive and healthier work environments demands innovation. Albert Einstein suggested this some time ago when he said: "The level of thinking that is required to get us out of the problems we have created is an order of magnitude greater than the thinking that got us into it." Transforming the global conditions that threaten our livelihood and our lives will require our sharpest, strongest skills. The first step is imagining the kind of world that we could live in.

Dr. Jonas Salk, in developing a methodology for researching his polio vaccine, once said that he "put away all facts and figures and tried thinking like a germ." He was not afraid to let intuition bring his imagination to bear on that epidemic scourge. His daring, combined with careful analysis and research, led him to a cure.

Dr. Salk had a reverence for intuition, which he described in his book *Anatomy of Reality*:

My mind is occupied by shifting patterns and changing relationships. I sense something strong and powerful that is acting
with interior as well as exterior force. I feel, as I feel the wind,
although I cannot see it. Forces of attraction act upon me;
they guide me as if I did not need a compass with which to
verify my course. I can only yield to the forces and move in
the direction toward which I am drawn, to a destination where
I have never been before.

He also knew the necessity of harnessing all his intellectual
and imaginative faculties to the task at hand:

Only by cultivating and refining the processes of intuition and
reason complementarily, only by reconciling them each in the
service of the other, can we achieve the wisdom we seek.

Building a Bridge to Imagination

To unlock the power of imagination, we often have to remove
the blinders of our conventional senses and/or the self-limiting
norms of our past experience. Explorer Ferdinand Magellan
first encountered native peoples along the coast of South
America when he anchored his great ships in the mouth of a
river harbor and rowed with his men in small boats to the
shore. There Magellan was greeted by a delegation from the local tribe who were mystified by the presence of the armored
strangers, and who asked by sign language how the voyagers
had traveled to their land. Magellan pointed at his ships in the
distance, but the natives could not see them. Ships of that size
were completely foreign to their experience, limited to their
sleek but relatively small canoes. The ships were unimaginable
and were therefore invisible to their eyes.

Italian cinematographer Federico Fellini said that "the visionary is the only true realist." In order to prepare our eyes to
envision something truly new, we need to maintain a connection between reason and imagination, to keep open the bridge
that conveys and supports the vehicle of creative action. In the
visible world, engineers build bridges. To build a bridge to
what we cannot see requires that we learn to be engineers of
the imagination. The next few sections describe ways in which
you can open yourself to the power of your imagination.

HEED YOUR DREAMS

All of us have known someone who has stated flatly, "I don't dream." We may even have said it ourselves at some point in our lives. Research shows that everyone dreams, so a more accurate statement would be that we have not found a way to recollect our dreams. When this happens, our consciousness is cut off from a highly imaginative source, which is also the foundation for personality.

Among American businesses, there are a number of companies whose corporate voice might also declare, "We don't dream." Such companies may have had a dream when they began, but once it was realized, employees become mired in the much less creative task of preserving a rigid vision, rather than seeking another. We do continue to dream but the dreamscape shifts. It is our responsibility to stay attentive and connected to the creative forces and places from which our dreams arise.

Rochelle Myers and Michael Ray are founders of the Creativity in Business seminar at Stanford's graduate business school. They have collected and published their experiences and insights from the seminar's first five years in a book entitled *Creativity in Business*. Stressing the need to be attentive to creative resources, Myers and Ray advise readers to "tune in to their dreams." There are many schools of dream interpretation, but Myers and Ray suggest that one does best by developing one's own method. "The point is to pay attention, and to understand that you are the total creator of your dreams and that the message comes from yourself." When we start to pay attention to our dreams, we begin to communicate with the limitless power of our own imagination and the messages that are generated within.

REGAIN WONDER

From a child's perspective, everything is possible. Barriers and limitations that introduce the specter of fear are not yet in place as they tend to be for adults. To learn a language, for example, is to experience the twin delights of sound and communication. A child is fluent no matter what her proficiency may be, because the language flows naturally from sound to speech to understanding. Adults often are so entangled in a thicket of rules for grammar and syntax that learning a new language is more like solving a crossword puzzle than gaining a living tool. Adults know that language can telegraph education and status—we want our speech to project a hard-won self-image, even if it means losing the ability to communicate in a desire to be correct. Years of wary speech have conditioned adults to be self-conscious when they speak, as if choosing the wrong word were a permanent embarrassment.

Because children are natural artists, they see everything vividly. A professor of English in upstate New York once wrote about taking his daughter to paint scenes of the lake near their home. One morning, painting her impression of a boat in full sail under a spring sky, his daughter set down brush strokes that were free and vigorous, the color vivid and evocative. Her intention was not to photograph the scene, but to put her heart and soul into it. You could feel rather than see the swelling sails of the boat as it carved a graceful path through the waters of the lake. Some days later, the girl was asked to create a picture of a sailboat for her school class. Her father suggested that she bring the one she'd made on their outing. Sadly, she explained that her teacher didn't like pictures like that, and she pulled out the dittoed assignment sheet that governed her project—two pale violet triangles on a box, sitting on a flat sea. Her job was to color this lifeless outline, and, as you might guess, to stay within the lines.

Picasso once remarked that every child is an artist, and the artist's challenge lay in remaining a child after one had matured. If we view business as an adult pursuit that requires "putting away childish things" and playing the game by constrictive rules, we pursue the things we know and miss discovering the things that we don't know.

SUCCEED BY BEING THE BEST AND MOST CREATIVE TRASH EMPTIER

We have inner potential to create ideas and invent what's necessary for optimum living. Discovering how to tap that source of power is a key to gaining a leading edge in our work and for our lives. Tapping that universal energy often poses a challenge for those pinned against the minor rib of a protective organizational umbrella.

One way to become the best at anything is to be innovative. No matter what level of task, we delude ourselves if we believe that we are giving it our best while closing off to innovation. Exciting possibilities are not the product of happenstance. Our own imagination helps to make them happen.

Second-generation entrepreneur Tony Garcia comes from a tradition of business leadership. Son of a part owner of the Philippines-based San Miguel Brewery, Garcia has himself, over the course of his career, owned and managed several firms, among them Bud's Ice Cream and A. F. Garcia Financial Traders. When he first graduated from college, armed with his business degree but little experience, his grandfather gave him valuable advice. Knowing that Tony would be starting somewhere very near the bottom of the corporate ladder, the older man offered several words of wisdom. "Don't be discouraged," he said, "when you expect to run the company, but your first job is to empty wastepaper baskets. Succeed by being the best and most creative trash emptier they ever had—the rest will follow."

Open Windows When Doors Close

According to Edward Hall in *Beyond Culture,* the answer to the world's most pressing problems does not lie in ordering or restricting human endeavor, but "in evolving new alternatives, new possibilities, new dimensions, new options, new avenues for creative use, [building upon] the unusual and multiple talents so manifest in the diversity of the human race."

Hall's ideal is one that many of us share. In many business contexts, however, that very creative impulse can be a most threatening one—and, therefore, is often the least encouraged. Because it often catalyzes change in what is already a chaotic sea of activities and decisions, creativity makes many solid citizens uneasy. Because it is a playful gift, it is criticized as a refuge for the immature. Envious people, rather than nurture someone else's creative idea, are paralyzed by the numbing question: "Why didn't I think of that?"

"Command-and-control management," which one writer has

caustically suggested was "invented by the Roman army and perfected by the Church" is a top-down style of business governance that historically leaves little room for imagination. When you join the firm, you get a congratulatory speech from the CEO and are handed a thick manual with policies and procedures. If you follow the rules and keep your nose clean, you are on track for promotion. If you do it long enough, there's a gold watch at the end of the trail.

Yet in the 1950s, corporate America flourished. This was a time when conformity was energized by the lion's share of the world's technology, a burgeoning consumer market, and an appetite for the spectacular. It is estimated that 50 percent of the world's innovation in manufacturing in the 1950s was generated by American business. Today, business observers believe that our world share of innovation is perhaps a tenth of what it was during those halcyon days. The reasons for the decline of America's preeminence in the world of business are not the subject of this book, but what needs to be said is that the principal gifts of the American temperament continue to be imagination, creativity, and the willingness to risk—to be leapers as well as builders. A respected Japanese automotive executive, Takashi Ishihara, once said that the Japanese consider Americans to be energetic, progressive, competitive, and always audacious enough to believe they can do something better or faster than the kid down the block. That imaginative, questing spirit is what Americans bring to the table in the global marketplace.

Transforming the Dragons, Tapping the Imaginative

In order to unleash the artist within, we first must transform the dragons of self-doubt that close us off from the realm of imagination. The dragons are easy to find: they are perched on the ramparts of every barrier to our creative center. They are fed by our fears and misconceptions of ourselves.

The dragons of fear and poor self-concept can cause us to make excuses to avoid the power of imagination. These are three of the most common excuses:

∞ I'm too old for new ideas.

∞ I don't have time.

∞ I know a better way, but I'm afraid to fail.

So let's debunk these myths right away: Certainly age is no hindrance to creativity; in fact, creativity is thought to peak in our mid-seventies. Alexander Graham Bell invented the telephone at age fifty-eight. George Bernard Shaw won a Nobel prize at seventy. Pulitzer Prize winner Wallace Stegner wrote some of his best work at eighty. Benjamin Franklin helped to write the Constitution at the age of eighty-one.

And neither is lack of time an excuse for not engaging in imaginative activity. The choice to use our time in ways that link us with imagination and its expression is always ours to make.

The prospect of failure, however, can interfere with our capacity to make the innovative choice, even though the world clearly progresses by experiment. "An inventor," observed General Motors' Charles Kettering, "is simply a person who doesn't take his education too seriously. If you flunk repeatedly in school, you're out. But an inventor is almost always failing. If he succeeds once, he's in. We often say that the biggest job we have is to teach a newly hired employee to fail intelligently." A batter in baseball also has far more failures than successes. Carl Yastremski had to stand at the plate ten thousand times in order to achieve three thousand hits.

HAVING NEW EYES

> The voyage of discovery lies not
> in finding new landscapes but in
> having new eyes.
>
> MARCEL PROUST

Often true originality does not mean birthing something entirely new but seeing fresh possibilities in what already exists. This can be as elaborate a discovery as the concept of *West Side Story*, which transforms the passions of Shakespeare's *Romeo and Juliet*, set in Renaissance Italy, into the star-crossed romance of teenagers in a tough New York City neighborhood.

Imagination let a timeless theme live again in a new way.

With a similar burst of imagination, Cookie Creations of Sacramento, a successful greeting service, successfully departed from the custom of sending traditional flowers to mark important occasions. Instead, the firm offers bouquets of chocolate chip cookies, to the delight of local and worldwide recipients.

Filling the Well Within

Creativity is a spiritual process that taps the abundance of a universe full of ideas. Imagination is like an inner well that flows according to its connection to the water source. Creativity has often been viewed in terms of water. Twelfth-century mystic Hildegard of Bingen referred to the Creator as "the purest spring" and Meister Eckhart's image was that of "a great underground river." It is perhaps not by coincidence that the necessary "greening of the earth's corporations" is related to the creativity required to transform an ever increasing desert once again into a lush, verdant forest. Any body of fluid, however, can become dry. A dried-up person or dried-up culture loses the ability to create. Thus discovering ways to tap the river of creativity for filling the well within are essential.

Here are some of mine:

∞ Music—I consider the significant amount of money that I spent replacing my portable tape player with a premier sound system to have been an investment. Early mornings are filled with the classical music of great musicians whose muse was the symphony of the cosmos, the sounds of the earth. Listening aligns my creative self to receive a flow of information and ideas. Just as everyone is an artist, so is everyone a musician also; the playing of a musical instrument is another way to nourish the inner well. Strumming a guitar, playing a keyboard or tapping out a drum rhythm draws us out of dry spells, placing us back on a creative path.

∞ Exercise—Daily exercise is not a routine; it is a blessing for the body. Not only do the muscle and organ systems of the body respond positively to the opportunity to move, but many of our best ideas come while we're engaged in a four-mile run or a brisk walk. As a river can become clogged with a log jam, a blocked flow of creativity can be jarred loose by moving the body and speeding up the heart. As the blood flows, so do the images and ideas that are waiting to be born.

∞ Writing—Keeping a daily journal inspires the creative juices. Freely writing down anything that flows from our conscious mind is a way to unblock sluggish thinking. I occasionally "blurt" onto a page what may seem like a crazy idea that later does not seem crazy at all. As a habit, I also write down dreams as possible road signs to a creative thought.

∞ Traveling—Journeying far from my usual surroundings often brings up new ideas. Novel places, people, and experiences can trigger a fresh perspective. With respect to the work world, a change of scenery can do wonders for a blocked imagination. In fact, occasional day trips in the middle of a pressured schedule may enhance productivity more than relentlessly forcing our head to the grindstone.

∞ Retreat—Twice each year I pack my computer, books, and dog and go to a completely different location to create. Although my home is a fine setting for an ongoing creative ritual, I find it helpful to change locations. I occasionally use a conference center where I work, eat, and sleep for two days even though the center is only fifteen miles from my home. The key to the retreat's success is the purposeful focus on creation.

∞ Serving Others—Whenever I feel my creative, giving spirit has been dampened, or I'm simply too tired to care, I drag myself out to serve someone else, thereby escaping my own ego. Giving the gift of our time and presence—working in a soup kitchen, reading to the blind, cleaning up litter, or refurbishing the home of someone in need—can be a significant contribution to the lives of others. In serving, we receive much more than we have donated—and what we receive, often, is a creative shot in the arm.

∞ Being Crazy—When all else fails, nothing gets your creative juices rolling faster than simply being crazy. When I let down my protective pretense and act like a playful, uninhibited child, I feel really alive. The brilliant and inspirational writer named SARK celebrates every moment of life. Here are some of her whimsical suggestions for being crazy:

> Eat mangoes naked, keep toys in the bathtub, send a love letter to yourself, wear pajamas to a drive-in movie, spin yourself dizzy, for one day hide all the clocks in your house, have a moonlight picnic, hug trees, make a blanket fort, invite someone dangerous to tea, draw on the walls, make little signs that say yes and post them all over your office or house, take a lot of naps!

A Creative Space

Where we create makes a difference. Participants in the EAGLES seminars find an image or work of art that reminds them of the inner management practice that they are to employ. They find one spot in their office to place the image. This creative spot can have family photos, mementos, award certificates, or a simple candle. Anything meaningful complements the creative spot, for meaningful items carry a historic energy that comforts, if not inspires, the imagination.

> When the creative spot has been set, it is important to approach the area with reverence and with ritual. As a preacher enters the pulpit in expectant silence or the priest approaches the altar trembling in awe, a leader approaches the creative spot with reverence because it will facilitate participation in the holiness of creation. We are about to encounter the sacred and from the encounter something original may result.

People frequently believe the creative life is grounded in fantasy. The more difficult truth is that creativity is grounded in reality, in the particular, the focused, the well-observed or specifically imagined.

As we lose our vagueness about our self, our values, our life situation, we become available to the moment. It is there, in the particular, that we contact the creative self. Until we experience the freedom of solitude, we cannot connect authentically. We may be enmeshed, but we are not encountered.

Art lies in the moment of encounter: we meet our truth and we meet ourselves; we meet ourselves and we meet our self-expression. We become original because we become something specific: an origin from which work flows.

JULIA CAMERON, *THE ARTIST'S WAY*

Simple Creative Rituals for Daily Life

Just as creative space, as an external environment, affects our imagination, creative ritual transforms our inner process, systematically awakening the creative self and promoting a full awareness of ourselves and our surroundings. Many of us have daily rituals; some contribute more to attentiveness than others. Working several simple principles into our routine will strengthen the bridge to imagination and spirituality.

BEGINNING THE DAY

When you emerge from sleep and your eyes first open, begin the day with an affirming phrase, prayer, or intention. Rather than jumping into "busyness," it is helpful to focus on the magnificence of "being" before "doing" begins.

BREATHING

The word inspiration takes its meaning from the Latin *in* + *spirare*, to breathe in. Take long, slow deep breaths that promote relaxation. Focus your breath throughout the day as a way of being attentive to your surroundings. Whenever chaos threatens, consciously breathe.

MOVEMENT

The ancient Chinese knew that physical movement integrates the body, mind, and spirit to subtly balance energy. Over centuries, they developed the deep movement practice of tai chi chuan. Its principles are universal. Even less formal and stylized rituals, such as adjusting our bodies so that we are sitting or standing properly, straighten the spine and promote creative attentiveness.

RELATING

When we meet each person, we can choose an attitude of acceptance or one of criticism. Acceptance of others for who they are, without judgment, is a mental ritual that brings enormous peace of mind and keeps you open for more creative action.

LIVING SIMPLY

Living simply is life's most essential—and often elusive—ritual. Simplicity is the thread binding all spiritual traditions. It is the bedrock of Amish and Buddhist life. When our lives become too burdened, our work becomes unfulfilling. By letting go our grip from material objects, we open our hands and heart to receive what is already present but unseen.

Work as Art

What we do is a measure of who we are. If we imagine our work as labor, we become laborers. If we imagine our work as art, we become artists. As Eric Gill has noted, "the artist is not a different kind of person, but every person is a different kind of artist." If that is true, it means that for some of us business is not only a profession, but a medium—just as painting, drawing, and sculpture are to the artist. Business, therefore can be an art form in which we address business problems not only with adult wisdom, but with a child's willingness to risk and create. In so doing, we participate in the ongoing process of creation.

How we discover the medium in which we will create is by first following our passion, for when we find our passion, we are on the path to discovering our true work. Passion, however, needs guidance. Directed by the wrong purpose, our work can become a contributor to our spiritual death. If directed by the purpose of serving, our work (and art) becomes a gift and our legacy.

WORKING WITH PASSION

> No man ever forgot the visitations
> of that power to his heart and brain,
> which created all things new; which
> was the dawn in him of music,
> poetry, and art.
>
> RALPH WALDO EMERSON

Passion is one of the most attractive of human characteristics. People naturally gravitate toward someone filled with passion. Passionate people love what they do because they have been courageous enough to do what they love. When we take the risk to do what we love, work becomes a vital expression of who we are.

I know several airline pilots, for example, who live to fly, to experience the feeling of soaring through the night in complete control of a powerful machine that gives wings to grounded human beings, and touching down in exciting ports of call after only a few hours in the air. My friends can hardly believe they are paid for such pleasure.

Passion Conquering Boredom

Even the most routine work can be driven by passion. I once read of a woman who packed light bulbs in cardboard sleeves for twenty-six years. It's hard to imagine a more stultifying occupation, but this woman transformed the work by treating it artfully and joyfully. She placed each bulb in its container swiftly yet with great care, and sent a silent blessing with every package, a wish that the user would benefit from the light that spread from that well-protected bulb. What she did fed her soul and sustained her in a routine occupation for a quarter-century. She had found a way to express love and care through her work, and it had become an extension of her being. She didn't regret Monday morning or long for Friday, nor did she view retirement as the time when she'd begin to live. She was finding a source for life in the process of work, a source of joy as illuminating as the bulbs she packed and blessed!

That kind of joy is much more rare than it ought to be. Whole populations can miss it altogether. I grew up in the small town of Schuylerville, New York, a town whose economy was dominated by a paper mill, and the haggard, resigned faces of the workers are etched in my mind.

Our family was exempted from the legacy of work at the mill. My father was a jeweler, and as such belonged to a different echelon in Schuylerville's social and economic hierarchy. He worked long hours, and rose every morning at 4:30 in order to work on watches for a few hours before he opened the store at 9:00 for a full day's business. His business prospered, and his life was perceived as different from those who worked at the mill. But what distinguished his work primarily was not the setting and certainly not the hours—it was the passion he found in practicing his art. I watched him peer into the delicate works of a fine watch through his jeweler's loupe, deftly placing and replacing tiny springs and screws with heads smaller than that of a pin. It was like working in a miniature universe, an intricate art form that carried with it an enormous sense of joy and accomplishment, as it called forth my father's skill and energy.

Reflecting on that time and place, I've come to believe it is essential for our work to incorporate a sense of passion and joy. We spend more than half our waking life at work, especially if we take it home from the office. Why shouldn't work be something we love, a joyful expression of art rather than a mechanical exercise of duty? The inner journey requires a balanced understanding of our being, but it also calls us to seek out work that springs from who we are. I consistently advise people who don't love what they do to get out of what they are doing and do what they love.

Passion Transformed into Beauty

I recently spent time in Paris, one of my favorite cities. At a farmer's market early one morning, we discovered that the display of food can be a true art and a feast for the eyes as well as the palate. Everywhere the produce had been set out and carefully arranged with exquisite symmetry and order. Bananas were stacked with their ripe yellow curves aligned for the most tempting view. Wicker bowls of tangerines and grapes flanked perfect pyramids of green beans and tomatoes. Scrubbed potatoes gleamed in their bins, alongside precise arrangements of onions and zucchini, like elements out of a Cezanne still life. The vegetables and fruits were arranged on green padding to simulate the spread of a meadow. In another part of the market, fish were placed with care on beds of ice. Farmers exhibited their produce with the same passion that people usually lavish on arranging photographs of their children. Never have I seen a more vivid example of work offered as art.

At a bakery on a Paris side street, we saw, smelled, and later tasted sculpted loaves dusted with flour and displayed in loving, exact geometries. Bread-making is a way of life in Paris; bread is meant to be experienced, not merely bought and consumed. This work is art for its own sake and a passion that is meant to be shared, an extension of the work of harvest, coupled with the artistic skill of baker, chef, and vintner.

Art Is Never Hurried

In her book *Slowing Down in a Speeded-up World,* Adair Lara describes how her mother washed clothes in an old-fashioned wringer washer and then hung them on the line to dry.

> As she pinned up each garment, she thought about the child it belonged to. (It was a wonder she knew; there were seven of us kids.) She never wanted a dryer, even after we could afford one, because it would steal this from her, this quiet contemplation.

Speed can be the natural enemy of art in work. Doing something quickly often robs us of the capacity to reflect on and appreciate the artistry of the work involved.

Art Is Festive

In his classic *Feast of Fools,* theologian Harvey Cox made this observation: "Preoccupied with producing and managing," he wrote, "[we] have lost touch with the vast reaches of reality. [Our] being has been borrowed and depleted. Therefore, festivity is not just a luxury of life. It provides the occasion for [us] to establish proper relation to time, history, and eternity."

To lead joyful lives through our work, we must become connected to festive passion, conscious that we are creating productive change, and aware that there are many ways to do the same thing.

WORKING WITH PURPOSE

My work as a pastor afforded me the rare privilege of sharing the intimate details of many people's lives. An average day could include the issues of death, birth, hope, and despair. Many of those people voiced concern about their life direction and the path they should follow. When I first began work as a pastor I actually tried to help them discern the correct path, giving more advice than was necessary. Some years later I asked myself that same question and the answer became very clear: The purpose of life is to give, not to receive.

Passing Through the Stage of Acquisition

Psychologist Carl Jung defined life in two stages, with a mid-life opportunity as the transitional state between the two. The first stage is a time of self-actualization when the ego stretches the boundaries in an effort to build a self-concept. During this stage many people have children, buy property, and acquire personal items that they believe reflect who they are. Young married couples receive gifts to start them on their way, buy a home, accumulate furniture, pets, cars, and eventually enough stuff to fill a garage and a basement. This is a necessary process as it fulfills certain needs that we, as flesh and blood, require. But our spirit eventually calls us to move from this stage. Journeying toward the predictable and necessary mid-life crisis, we begin to examine the lack of meaning in acquiring material things and instead of asking what, how, or when, we start to ask why.

Many people, however, when confronted with this mid-life opportunity, remain unwilling to move toward change. Money, sex, and power remain the icons of success and of supreme importance in modern society. If we remain in the first stage of life, these become the dominant forces behind our behavior and prevent us from finding our true purpose.

Moving Beyond Ego

When we in the Patnaude Training Group teach people the Art of Speaking, we help them overcome one of life's greatest fears. The key to that change lies in a new perception. Instead of intending to get something from an audience, i.e. applause, approval, or affirmation (which are all needs related to fear of failure), the speaker must focus on giving to the audience. When the speaker's intention is to serve the needs of listeners by informing and motivating them, the dynamic changes. The speaker gives, and when there is no need to receive, the giving is returned many times over.

The manager who gives her time to coach others into more responsible and productive work behaviors will benefit greatly. A deep sense of satisfaction is experienced by giving the employee the opportunity to actualize their agreed-upon goal. Instead of exacting results upon demand, work is planned and delegated, productivity usually is higher and stress is reduced as others are empowered to contribute to the whole. It is indeed, "more blessed to give than to receive," but it takes a new orientation to begin the process.

I interviewed a leader of a small, very successful company whose standard question to all his employees was, "What can I do to help you?" Instead of maintaining a directive role by telling people what to do, he saw his job as helping others be successful in what they did. He became a staff person to them and served as their greatest support.

WORK AS A GIFT

Henry Frankel, president and founder of Frankel Industries Incorporated, a New Jersey company that recycles plastics, is a man who embodies the concept of work as art. Because he works to serve others, his work is its own reward. Henry doesn't work to gain awards, he works toward a goal about which he is passionate. Recognition and financial success were by-products of working with love and out of gratitude; they were not Henry's primary goal.

If we see our life orientation as one of service, we begin to let go of the need for material things. When we seek to simplify our lives, travel more, acquire less, and enjoy the benefits of simplicity, we experience the freedom to serve, which is the ultimate of gifts.

A Passion for Using All Resources

Henry Frankel has had a passion for recycling reusable materials since he was six years old. Escaping from Hitler's Germany in 1940, Henry made his way to the United States safely on a children's transport, an Italian ship whose precious cargo was the lives of Jewish children who escaped death and found passage to a new life. Under the direction of a program of the German Jewish Aid Society, Henry was placed in the home of an American family. When his mother was able to escape a year later, Henry was reunited with her and they began their new life in America. His father died in the concentration camps.

Henry aided in the war against the Third Reich by forming the Junior Commandos who, identified by arm bands, pulled their carts through the neighborhoods of New York collecting tin cans, scrap iron and steel, and cooking fat. The metal was used for crafting new machines of war that would defeat the Nazis— even the glycerin in the cooking fat aided in bomb production. Little did Henry know that he was setting a foundation for a career that would make a difference in the global environment a generation hence.

Henry attended the City College of New York, which he considers a gift afforded to him by the generosity of his new country. He went on to Leigh University, eventually becoming a manufacturing engineer, which led him to a path of efficiency and conservation in business as he learned the most prudent path was using the least amount of material in the shortest amount of time.

Henry believes that there are no accidents and that his focus is the result of certain events that awakened his consciousness. The energy crisis of 1974, for example, made him realize how limited the resources of the planet actually were. When he joined IBM in Burlington, Vermont, in 1965 he soon discovered that they needed his ideas and passion if they were to recover the cost of the excessive waste typical of development organizations. Although IBM had an energy conservation policy on the books, it had not been successful in recycling usable materials. When charged by his authorities to respond to the challenge, Henry turned in results at a pilot plant that saved 19 percent of the resources in the first year. Material resource management became his new focus; Henry's art quickly became known in IBM's thirty-six plants worldwide. Henry received the Outstanding Innovation Award for his achievements; clearly, his contribution was making a difference.

Henry left IBM to follow his passion and started his own business. Beginning with the collection of plastic drums that were recycled for building floating docks in the crystal clear waters of Lake Champlain, Frankel Industries was born. In 1990, while serving as an assistant professor at the Center for Packaging Science and Engineering at Rutgers University, he won the Zenith Master of Innovation Award for his accomplishments in developing automatic sorting techniques. He created a computer system that integrates hardware, software, and sensors to operate and manage automated facilities for sorting recyclable plastic containers. The program's Windows and multitasking functions also allow for simultaneous bookkeeping and quality control while driving the sorting line. Frankel's innovation, the "Kiss Spotlight System," enables the recycling of 85 percent of commonly used thermal plastics. The process allows a profit and provides an avenue for aiding our resource-worn planet.

Henry says, "I owe my life to strangers. An American family took my mother and me in when we were refugees. I was educated at the expense of the American people and my desire is to give back as much as I can."

Henry Frankel is an artist. Following the passion of his childhood heart, with a purpose and desire to serve and assist humankind, his work is a gift to all of us who share residence on this fragile planet.

5 INTUITION

> I want to be with those who know
> secret things, or else alone.
>
> RAINER MARIA RILKE

THE CENTER OF THE MAZE is where we receive intuitive wisdom. It is the place of silent retreat for the executive who is in the process of fashioning a vision that is just one step away from clarity. It is the laboratory arena that entertains a divine intelligence beyond human wisdom for the scientist who seeks a cure for a life-threatening disease. It is the place of quiet inspiration for every person who has journeyed inward and left excess baggage along the path. It is the place of the heart that, in its holiness, confirms the images of the mind as true.

It was through the application of Carl Jung's work *Psychological Types*, first published in 1922, that psychology's pioneers Katherine C. Briggs and her daughter, Isabel Briggs-Myers, discovered that 75 percent of the population processes data through the use of the five senses. For most of the world, seeing is believing. The remainder of the populace prefers relying on their intuitive skills for the processing of information. These people understand that believing is seeing as they trust their sixth sense and beyond. The attentive intuitive is one who is able to know the unknowable, to reach beyond the limits of the human senses into the realm of the divine and know, as Rilke said, "secret things."

Our minds know what they know and usually what they don't know as well. When we limit our knowing to only what we deem feasible through our sensory intakes, we remain at a level far below our potential and are unable to recognize data from beyond those limitations. If we allow ourselves to function as multi-sensory beings, we open a door to unlimited wisdom that resides outside the realm of knowledge based solely on our five senses.

Moving Aside Dragons

The dragons of the maze, predictably, stand in the way of this new wisdom; fear of the unknown is a primary obstacle. Because fear can create behavior that demands control over what we don't know, have, or understand, we take on the mentality of scarcity, which proclaims that if we are to have what we need, we must hold on to what we have. Unfortunately, that which we want most is lost in the desire to control. A parent who attempts to control her or his children out of fear of losing them, paradoxically can lose the child by suffocating her or him. Conversely, parents who view their children as the most special guests of their lives and who create a living room of love, trust, and hope through which their offspring pass, will forever savor an indescribable intimacy with their children. Recognizing and transforming this fear of loss is the first step toward deepening human relationships. The recognition and transformation of fear of the unknown is essential if we are to create an environment of love, trust, and hope. Thus, the maze's center, after the simplifying process of the journey inward, becomes that living space—once free of the clutter of fear it can host the infinite. As William Blake wrote:

If the doors of perception were cleansed, everything would appear as it is, infinite.

Blending the Sensory and Intuitive

Any leap into the unknown requires some cognitive data before you jump. If you are about to leap off a pier, there is some comfort in knowing that there's water below and that it's deep enough to break your fall. Some people on the pier need more data than others—the temperature of the water, the effect of the tide, whether there's a ladder to get back to dry land. Others need far less, but it's unwise to make the leap before you've gathered all the available data.

Intuition leads us to additional sources of unexpected information and may provide the final push that empowers us to make the jump. Eventually every leader has to discover sufficient trust to jump into the realm of the unknown. To avail ourselves of this powerful resource, we need to develop a taste for adventure, to seek an awareness of what seems unknowable.

APPLYING INTUITION IN BUSINESS

The seven last words of any organization are "But we've always done it this way." Two words that give us access to the new world are "What if...?" Every business decision calls upon the power of imagination to allow new realities to permeate the old at many levels.

Because the majority of us depend upon our five senses, it is not surprising that American business leaders are encouraged to be gregarious, appreciative of the scientific method, hungry for consummating the sale, and respectful of the bottom line. It is also not surprising that the business community is suspicious of introverts, dreamers, and intuitives. Introverts are labeled as shy if they are valuable to the company and antisocial if they're not. Such employees are tolerated if success proves them to be visionaries but more often are dismissed as simply impractical. Similarly, people who rely on intuition are seen as exciting, but perhaps, just a little frightening as they depend on "secret things" to guide their course.

The practice of assigning a social, economic, or moral value to personality traits means that we can reduce those traits to clichés, which leads to the assumption that we don't need to explore them, whether they appear in others or lie inside ourselves (as they do), waiting for discovery. The common shorthand for intuition is "playing hunches." Therefore, the intuitive who "stumbles" on an original conclusion or idea is seen as being nothing more than lucky. Everybody feels lucky at one time or another, so intuition, unfortunately, becomes a synonym for the kind of sly prescience that allows a gamble to pay off once in a while.

Several years ago I took my two daughters, Julie and Laura, to the horse races. Being horse lovers we not only enjoyed the beauty of the animals but played the game of betting on our favorite horse with equal enthusiasm. In the first two races, we examined all the data for each horse and jockey, noting their ages, earnings, and ratings. After all information was assessed, we made our choice based on the data and sat back to watch our diligent efforts pay dividends. They didn't. In both races, our choice didn't even place. At that point I suggested to my children that we narrow the choices to the top five horses based on record and then intuitively select our bet according to an inner feeling. We won the next five races. The bigger prize was being reminded to use all resources when taking a chance.

The cynic would say that our choices were just lucky guesses. I think more than luck is involved but pinning down exactly what intuition is can be difficult. Here's a short list of both what it is and what it is not:

∞ It's knowing the unknowable: The great French painter Henri Matisse wrote: "In art, truth and reality begin when one no longer understands what one is doing or what one knows, and when there remains an energy that is all the stronger for being contained... Obviously it is necessary to have all of one's experience behind one, but to preserve the freshness of one's instincts."

∞ It's wisdom, not data: The Tao Te Ching notes: "He who thinks he knows, does not know. He who knows that he does not know, knows."

∞ It's articulated feeling, not conscious thought: Intuition swoops up from the unconscious like the mistral wind of

Provence, so powerful as to take one's breath away, so insistent that the timid process of thought becomes all but impossible.

∞ It's oral, not written communication: Taking their cue from the Hellenistic philosophers, the Roman Empire deified the power of the written word. All wisdom was of the book. Writing domesticates the untamed energy of traditions that were once so deep that they could only be whispered to initiates in the night, who then gave birth to wild ideas that danced in the firelight. Not all that is worth knowing can be written down. Intuition is the news that's not fit to print, but is essential to learn.

At those times when we are most clearly aware that we've tapped into that inner voice, there is also a certain confidence that builds inside, an excitement that goes beyond knowledge or trust in the product. It's as if you can see beyond what you have in hand or as if you have suddenly acquired the ability to know the unknowable. This is the realm of intuition, the creative manifestation of blind optimism, knowing you've got all the pieces, including a heretofore missing piece which you can only just now sense.

Intuition, what Emerson called the "blessed impulse," is the gateway to a different way of knowing, but in the day-to-day world of business life, it cannot function effectively apart from reason. Left-brained thinking—logical, analytical, technical—is not only an acceptable way to do business, but is both necessary and admired. However, in today's volatile business climate, not everything can be achieved by such controlled patterns of thought. Room must be made for that rarely understood combination of life experience, knowledge, and instinct that gives rise to intuition.

Mark Twain once said of the ancient art of river piloting: "Two things seemed apparent to me. One was that in order to be a pilot, a man has got to learn more than any man ought to be allowed—and the other was that he must learn it all over again every twenty-four hours." The periodic floods of an enraged and unpredictable Mississippi and its sister rivers have demonstrated the truth of that need for double wisdom—all that is known and all that is newly to be known. It is also a perfect symbol for the white water world of commerce, where the challenges demand both a thorough knowledge of the past and an ability nimbly to confront the future. The former requires research and analysis, the latter courage and intuition.

A Laboratory for Intuitive Design

Sara Little Turnbull has been Director of The Process of Change, Innovation, and Design Laboratory at Stanford University since the laboratory was founded.

To release intuition, Sara believes that one must first have a deep sense of caring. When we care we become connected with the subject of concern. It evokes our passion and our attentiveness. When students arrive to work with Sara she frequently shocks them with intuitive insights she has regarding them. She attributes this insight partially to knowing her material, but sees its primary source as the affinity she has for the students. Sara stresses that one must know a great deal about the subject—caring is not a shortcut to avoid research. Intuition is like the frosting on the cake. It's preceded by a lot of elbow grease, a lot of effort, a lot of honing. It is not magic but often the result of very hard work.

Sara also stresses the danger of believing you already know what you need to know:

> When students come to the lab, they expose a very particular and personal kind of vulnerability. I get the very strong and I get the very weak. I get the ones who come in here strong enough to be vulnerable and to say 'There is a kind of experience I need to have before I can understand what I want to do with my project.'
>
> The very weak are the ones who come in and say, 'I know exactly what I want to do.' With that kind of thinker, there's just one little chink of light that comes through that façade. They want to see whether they are placed securely enough, whether they've looked at a broad enough base. That's [also] a very healthy time to come into the lab. It's what you do with the information, the idea of browsing and developing your own path.

Applying Intuition in Business

At a recent EAGLES seminar, several executives and entrepreneurs discussed a range of applications for intuition in their businesses, including the interview process, making business decisions when there are "holes in the facts," strategic visioning, and product design.

∞ As a teenager, product engineer Bob Lorenzini (whose story was discussed in Chapter Two) designed a part to convert the tank shift of his ancient motorcycle to a more modern and convenient foot shift. The intuitive dimension of that project fueled his interest for innovative solutions ever afterwards, the latest being a design for a crystal growing furnace. His appreciation of the needs of operation and maintenance caused a simple design to emerge from his intuition—a furnace that was efficient, yet easy both to assemble and take apart.

∞ In a similar context, LanDec Corporation founder Ray Stewart, a leading innovator in chemical research, used available information, hunches, and internalized experience to conjecture accurately how a new polymer would behave, producing a material that would manifest two distinct and essential properties when all analysis suggested one would be lost. No computer was capable of flashing on its monitor what Ray had allowed himself to say inside, where only he could hear: "Try this!"

∞ A securities firm manager sounded a more somber note about the cost of not heeding one's intuition. He recalled interviewing a candidate for a job. He had asked the right questions, and had gotten the right answers. Yet something was not quite right. "We all had an intuition about it," he said, "but didn't share it. Each of us had heard a small voice whisper, 'Don't hire this person'! His qualifications appeared impeccable, his personality acceptable. Only afterward did we find that he had not graduated from the University of Texas as he had claimed, and he had not been a VP in his previous firm but rather a middle manager. This served to put his personality into question as well."

∞ Norman Tu parlayed his intuition into an immensely successful service. His company, DisCopy Labs, copies disks and computer files. He received a request to have workstation cartridges duplicated. Whereas a standard copy might take ten minutes, these memory monsters of 30 to 40 megabytes required at least an hour to complete. The decision to accept that contract was based on an intuition that this "might be big," not a market mandate. After following his intuition to fulfill this request, it soon became apparent that major industry players—Sun, SGI, IBM—all needed the service. The single contract grew to a $5 million business segment in three years, and catapulted Norman's firm to the national lead in disk copy service. Other decisions, conscientiously based on market studies, have paled by comparison.

According to Unilever chairman F. A. Maljers, "strategy at corporate level must build upon the strategies at lower levels in the hierarchy, while at the same time all parts of the business must work to accommodate corporate goals. The requirement [or the strategic planner] is to find the right equilibrium.... The real dynamic and highly competitive world of business places great demands on all scarce resources, especially time." Therefore, Maljers reports, strategic decisions are based on experience and intuition, as well as thorough analysis.

Intuitive Health Care

Rachel Naomi Remen, M.D., uses intuition and teaches other doctors how not to block their own intuition. Assistant Clinical Professor of Family and Community Medicine at the School of Medicine at the University of California, San Francisco, Remen teaches medical students ways to tap into the intuitive mind for diagnosing the needs of their patients. Learning to trust the inner voice (which often communicates through feelings rather than intellect), doctors can often tap a knowing that is beyond their acquired knowledge. Using the intuitive in psychotherapy is a way of helping patients heal as they learn to quiet their mind and open their heart to the wisdom that may bring about a transformation of their dragons.

Intuition is a different level of communication from our most common interactions. All of us receive intuitive messages constantly but often don't register them because most of the time our minds are busy with staff meetings, daycare, or getting to the dry cleaner before it closes. In our culture, the behavioral norm is based on doing, whereas intuition requires an attentiveness to being, and a consciousness that can discern the still, quiet voice.

Imagine what our organizations would be like if we recognized the intuitive personality. Project teams could rely on intuitive guidance. Every CEO could follow the example of King Arthur and use a "Merlin-in-residence" for discerning trends, future clients, and strategic visioning. Managers could use intuition as the final word in hiring personnel. Such leadership requires courage and a willingness to tap all sources of wisdom, apparently the norm for Unilever chairman, F. A. Maljers:

> The combination of uncertain time horizons and unavoidable time and resource pressures lead to an important role for intuition within the formulation of business strategy. Intuition is a vital and integral part of thinking. It gives the benefit of a holistic approach to problem solving, and reflects the value of cumulative experience.

6 JOY

To love life through our labor is
to be intimate with life's inmost
secrets.

KAHLIL GIBRAN

JOY FINDS FULL EXPRESSION IN ARTIST, entrepreneur, and micro-venture capitalist Jacques Littlefield. His remarkable hilltop horse ranch features not thoroughbreds, but one of the world's largest collections of armored vehicles. With a workshop and work force that a genuine army would envy, Littlefield and his staff spend endless hours refitting this collection of historical pieces for an eventual museum to be built on the property. Occupying much of the ranch property is another set of tracks laid out for a seven-and-a-half-inch gauge train that guests can actually ride. A fifty-member club meets monthly to build new railroad cars and maintain the rail system itself as a hobby. Evenings at the ranch often feature organ concerts in the Littlefield's performance hall, constructed under Jacques's express directions and housing a Fisk organ that many appraisers consider to be one of the best built in the twentieth century. Curious visitors are warmly welcomed by a man who knows no limits.

Sound like the opulent life of modern royalty? Hardly. Jacques and his wife Liz are the parents of three children and are as solid as the ground that supports their antique tank collection. Nourishing a spiritual life by singing in the local church choir and serving on four nonprofit boards is only possible because Jacques manages his time. He works from 7:30 A.M. to 1:00 P.M. each day at his financial investments and then devotes his afternoons to tanks, trains, and ranch-related tasks. When asked to describe his dream for what he will have accomplished ten years hence, Littlefield replies, "Staying on course, walking the steady path and doing just what I am doing." Leaving the ranch, one experiences the overwhelming joy embodied in a man whose life is fully expressed.

How can more leaders follow Littlefield's example? For many of us with great responsibilities, life is not fully expressed and instead becomes a tedious routine. Excessive stress, depression, and dysfunction often become the norm. Stuck in the past of the wounded child or the victimized adult, the joyless traveler lacks the understanding or desire to move beyond inertia.

The experience of joy produces psychochemicals that are health-protecting and life-enhancing. These brain-generated drugs, endorphins, are two hundred times stronger than morphine, yet all of their side effects are healthy. Endorphins produce a feeling of euphoria that is unlike all other human experiences and give us a taste of the life fully expressed. Designed to overcome the chemicals of fear that the body generates, endorphins are only released by the brain when we are able to break the stress and depression cycle related to the difficulty of surviving in a harsh world. When this occurs, we actually begin to feel the psychochemistry related to joy. Joy, in contrast to survival, is transcending normal living to reach an intense awareness of being alive and celebrating each step of the way.

The late Joseph Campbell, a prodigious authority on comparative mythology, used the word "bliss" to describe the constant joyful sense that animates the most meaningful human journeys. In the transcript of his celebrated interviews with Bill Moyers, published as *The Power of Myth*, he said that to "follow your bliss" means:

To put yourself on a kind of track that has been there all the while, waiting for you, and the life that you ought to be living is the one you are living … Follow your bliss and don't be afraid, and doors will open where you didn't know they were going to be. Religious people tell us we really won't experience bliss until we die and go to heaven. But I believe in having as much as you can of this experience while you are still alive.

Joy in Work

In Sinclair Lewis's novel *Babbitt,* George Babbitt is the epitome of an apparently solid businessman of the 1920s who has sacrificed his soul on the altar of progress and boosterism. He is the Faustus of the American dream. At the end of the novel, Babbitt's son tells him that he wants to forego school and work as an auto mechanic—simply because he loves it. Even though Babbitt's own ambition is to see his son earn a college degree, he gives him his blessing, because, as he says, "I have never done a single thing that I wanted to in my whole life." His successes are no more satisfying to him than ashes because he has never given himself permission to seek and taste joy in his life or in his work. In his struggle to survive, life and work were labors to endure rather than celebrate; Babbitt's tragedy is that he never pursued what he loved. But a key axiom of a way of knowing is that we must do what we love. Only within this context can we discover the true meaning of joy.

Great philosophers have always been aware of the deep, intimate connection between who we are and what we do. Thomas Merton, who combined the unlikely professions of contemplative monk and celebrated writer, encouraged people to ask him what he did, and to push him for clarity, because it was a measure for him of who he was. He had learned to love both the active and contemplative sides of his nature and knew also the intimate and essential relationship between doing and being.

WORK-RELATED MYTHS

There are many work-related myths that prevent us from connecting the worlds of being and doing and thus experiencing joy in work.

∞ It's just a job!

∞ I work only in order to live.

∞ Work is not meant to be fun.

∞ What I love and what I do don't have to coincide.

∞ What I believe and what I do don't have to coincide.

∞ Choose one career and stay with it.

A Joy-in-Work Inventory

Determining the true purpose of our work is the key to discovering joy in what we do. If we work to create ways in which we can further destroy our planet or each other, it is immoral. If our work only feeds our addiction for more and more material things, it is unhealthy. If our work exploits others and diminishes human potential, it is unjust. If our work is to be our art, it must pass the test of being a gift to all who encounter our legacy.

Every organization must ask itself: Do those who work here leave better, wiser, healthier, more empowered than when they began? If not, then we have just created another environment that suppresses human potential rather than provide a place in which the spirit soars. As a part of our contribution to being a co-creator of joyful workplaces, we can ask ourselves the following questions:

1. Is my work a contribution? Does it make a difference? Will I leave a legacy?
2. Is there a rhythm to my work that is natural, balanced, and steady rather than frantic and irregular?
3. Can I enjoy a routine of simple tasks associated with my greater vision and perform that work with equal regard?
4. Do I contribute toward fulfilling the needs of society or, am I contributing toward creating need?
5. Do I contribute toward creating a healthy and whole work climate as a result of my behavior and my attitude?
6. Do I treat each person with equal respect for who he or she is and what he or she contributes?

Such questions can begin the process of discovering our true purpose and can reorient us toward discovering one of life's true loves.

Joy in Play

In our seminar, Journey to Inner Excellence, we always have a five-foot-high medicine ball sitting outside the door of our training room. It is so large that people who pass by have to maneuver around it. Although only used for thirty minutes in the afternoon of the second day of the workshop, the ball is a silent proclamation that the action inside the room near where it sits is playful.

If you ask a child who has spent hours with friends playing in the woods, exploring caves, or building a stone bridge over a stream what he was doing all afternoon, you most likely will hear the response, "nothing!" A "nothing" response from a child probably indicates that the activities that filled the entire afternoon were as natural as breathing. Nothing means, "we were playing." Adults, on the other hand, seem to judge play as neither serious nor useful. Recreation is acceptable but play is childish. The seminar participants who play with the medicine ball first have to overcome guilt that they are playing with a large, colorful ball, on company time, in a field in full view of the company and the CEO's office.

Developmental theory indicates that play is a necessity for the growth and learning of a child. From the first game of peek-a-boo, the child is poised to engage in the world of play. I also remember the daily trip to the door of my friend's house to ask the inevitable question, "Can Billy come out and play?" We had no agendas but knew (in the way of knowing possessed by children) that if we hung around together the experience of play would simply happen. Many adults have lost the courage to ask friends to "come out and play." For an adult, play must have rules, competition, and a reward in order to justify time away from busy schedules. Because the goal of play for adults is to be the best and win, adults get discouraged when they play "badly." In corporate boardrooms some play "hardball" or "for keeps," but such interpretations skew the true meaning of play. A challenge to leadership is to discover the relationship between the playful child and the play-acting adult, the realm of make-believe and belief, a child's toys and adult toys, and playful vision and strategic vision. Uniting the worlds of work and play opens the door to the possibility of playful work.

Philosopher Alan Watts expressed this sentiment perfectly:

> I happen to like archery—not for killing things, but as a sport. What I like most all is to set free an arrow like a bird. It climbs high into the sky, then suddenly turns and drops. What is it that fascinates me about that? I am delighted by it because it's not useful. It doesn't really achieve anything that we could call purposive work. It is simply what we call play. But in our culture we make an extremely rigid division between work and play. You are supposed to work in order to earn enough money to give you sufficient leisure time for something entirely different called having fun or play. This is a most ridiculous division.

Why is it that we can feel such tension between the worlds of work and play and think that anything fun cannot be work?

THE BENEFITS OF PLAY

True play nourishes the self. Like the winter rains that fill a reservoir dried from overuse, a child instinctively goes about play naturally, filling an inner need for wonder, creating, and celebrating.

Play, according to the dictionary, is recreation, a word that, when hyphenated, becomes re-creation. Thus play means to make new, to inspire, to re-create; every experience that provides this opportunity is play. However, play is not the act itself of building blocks or climbing trees but primarily an attitude we create that becomes woven into the fabric of our lives. Although we schedule events to provide a vehicle for fulfilling our needs for self-nourishment, it is not the event itself that is play but the attitude we bring to the event. We can attend the year's greatest party, but if we don't want to be there, we can bet our dance cards will not be filled.

Plato said "Life must be lived as play," a reminder to approach life with an attitude of celebration. Certainly all of life's turns in the maze are not playful events, yet how we approach the shadows and the dragons makes a major difference in how we transform them. The attitude of play is that which transforms the dutiful into the divine, the required into the desired, and the boring into the joyful. The attitude of play means playing without purpose. The moment play takes on a purpose—weight control, competition, health, looks, gambling—it loses it truest meaning.

MASSAGING HARDENED ATTITUDES

Discovering the opportunity for playful work means softening attitudes that have hardened over time. If we can return to what was not only valued but necessary as a child learner, we can open the door to unlimited possibilities in our work. Consider bringing a bag of marshmallows to add a playful atmosphere to often tense and long staff meetings. Simply throwing soft white projectiles is a wonderful release. Standing ovations, at any time, are another way to change the climate of a room almost instantaneously. Try jumping to your feet and leading the room in giving some deserved person a standing ovation (hoots and cheers included), and watch what happens.

Reaping Joy from Pain

One of the aspects of joy that may seem most enigmatic is pain—a gift that few are able to recognize. Western society is more intent on avoiding pain than embracing it, thus the proliferation of drugs and chemicals that mask it from our conscious reality. Yet pain and pleasure are Siamese twins. Leonardo da Vinci sketched a male figure split in two, with two torsos, two heads, and four arms as his rendition of the Allegory of Pleasure and Pain with the following comment: "Pleasure and pain are represented as twins, as though they were joined together for there never is one without the other."

The paradox is that pain is a dimension of joy. Although we more readily associate joy with happiness, joy instead is that dimension of life expressed in fullness, which inevitably includes pain. Life without struggle and pain is a life unobserved.

THE STAGES OF PAIN

In any pain cycle, there are three stages to the learning process. Stage one is that of the signal. We are alerted that something is wrong. As a three-year-old, I distinctly remember picking up a red hot andiron that had fallen over in a fireplace containing a roaring fire. The second stage is that of the message, which for me as a three year old was, "this is hot!" Stage three involves the response, which happens rather quickly when you are holding a flesh-burning object. When we become attentive to pain in terms of this natural process, we can begin to manage pain in relationships, at work, and in our solitary behavior.

WAYS TO PUT PAIN IN PERSPECTIVE

One of my mentors was a tiny yet powerful woman named Helen. In addition to enduring problems with her children that would have leveled most of us, she was a victim of acute arthritis. At any given time she would be suffering from three vertebrae fractures painful enough to immobilize anyone but her. Her hands were so disfigured she could hardly open the door yet she greeted me joyfully and welcomed me into an atmosphere of pleasure and intrigue. Helen eventually died from a rotation of her spine so radical that her heart was punctured by a rib bone. In spite of her unimaginable physical pain, never, in the times I was with her did I ever hear one syllable of complaint, one expression of remorse. She was deepened by her pain and radiated joy in concert with it.

> With the help of the thorn in my
> foot
> I spring higher than anyone with
> sound feet.
>
> SØREN KIERKEGAARD

Think of Pain Endured Voluntarily

All of us endure some pain voluntarily. Women who wear high heels, pluck eyebrows, or wax their legs undergo discomfort for the sake of fashion. Athletes endure punishing blows to their bodies, and body builders champion the philosophy, "No pain, no gain." If we are willing to undergo pain for desirable ends, why does involuntary pain seem so unmanageable?

Laugh, Play, Heal

A study in England proved that hospitalized patients who could see trees from their windows healed faster from surgery than those unable to see outdoors. We have learned that laughter, color, music, and touch all make a difference in the healing process and in the management of pain.

Remember the Benefits of Pain

One of my clients is in a high-level position in a division previously headed by a Machiavellian vice-president who would thunder proclamations from above, the division walked very quietly and fearfully around him. Key elements of the work climate? Fear, suspicion, and mistrust. Significantly, it was not until the tragic death of a manager's brother that the atmosphere began to change. Compassion took the place of fear as everyone reached out to this devastated young woman. When two more deaths occurred within three months—including the death of one of the company's key secretaries, who died at home alone—the division and the raging king were brought to their knees. With tears of deep sadness and yielding spirits, the VP and his managers together met with a counselor to share their grief and confusion. Although the VP would soon move on to another position, the organizational climate began a profound change as trust, openness, and vulnerability became acceptable norms and the foundation for future leadership. Here, pain had actually been the catalyst that propped a brick in a closing door of opportunity.

When we learn not to fear pain but instead embrace it as a teacher, we can even change the behavior that causes the pain. This is an occasion for joy as we continue a process for growing into our potential.

Sharing Pain

Being surrounded by the people we love can transform even the most devastating pain. I shared the pain of an executive VP of one of the country's most esteemed advertising agencies when he and his wife tragically lost their twelve-year-old son. I was deeply moved as I listened to this man eulogize his child with a personal conviction and power that came from the deepest recesses of his soul. Thanking many hundreds of business associates who attended the memorial, he said that he had drawn strength from their love, presence, and the work lives they had shared together. Many of us at that service will be forever changed by his words. Life and work need not be separated; they are part of a whole.

Helen Keller said, "I am grateful for my handicap." Spirits like hers set an example of changing inner attitudes in order to change the outer aspects of our lives.

Joy in Community

I have emphasized the power of community and its transforming effect on pain. Because pain is inevitable and one of the teachers in the realm of joy, our challenge for living a joy-filled life is to develop multiple communities around us. Like it or not, we spend more waking hours with the people at work than we do with our families. If we learn to enjoy our co-workers as a community of fellow travelers, it can become a most important collection of people who love us, support, and challenge us toward the living of a life fully expressed.

Alexis de Tocqueville, in 1835, in his work *Democracy in America,* described American culture as having unique "habits of the heart," with our most impressive characteristic being individualism. Our habit of individualism, however, was positive only if balanced by other habits; otherwise, he warned, we would become isolationists and a fragmented society. Robert Bellah, in his book *Habits of the Heart,* written 150 years later, indicates that we have ignored that warning and become a fragmented society characterized by individualism. If we are to survive on this planet, Bellah warns, we must learn to live as a community, for "without it, indeed, there may be very little future to think about at all."

Although this book focuses primarily on work and the inner life of the individual, it is for the purpose of ultimately sharing these inner gifts within the context of community. When each participant brings ingredients to share in the making of "stone soup," a simple broth becomes a rich and nourishing stew. The path to transformation of organizations, systems, or a planetary society must begin within the heart of the individual; that awakened heart becomes the foundation of the communal phase of the labyrinth, a way of action. When we join with others, the flame of the heart becomes a roaring fire and, possibly, an eternal flame.

I see a great hunger for community in all places where I work. In the eyes of the participants with whom I have the privilege of working, I discover a desire to be known and to be loved, to be appreciated and touched, challenged and moved. They come to learn but their deepest desire is to be known.

The true spirit of community is one of cooperation, not competition. On October 19, 1989, my daughters and I sat in a home near San Francisco that rolled and shook at a level beyond our previously limited imagination as we experienced the most destructive earthquake in California since 1906. A city dedicated to individualism was instantly transformed into a community of cooperation as millions of people coalesced to help one another. Many of the businesses in the area offered help to those who most needed it. For example, two days after the quake, IBM and many other companies asked all their employees not affected by the quake to report to work in jeans, ready to deliver goods and services to other members of their community. Computer salespeople delivered blankets, clothing, and can openers to stranded people in Watsonville. Systems analysts manned impromptu information desks to answer questions and provide services for people in the devastated Marina district who couldn't get into their homes. In a time of crisis, with genuine compassion, people reached out to touch and talk, lift and listen, care and cooperate as we began the process of rebuilding. We returned to live our lives behind our private walls only after the crisis had passed and the memory faded, hopefully more awakened to the potential of what could be as a result of the experience of what was.

The experience of community is one of true joy. Schuylerville, New York, where I grew up, was once an idyllic village nestled in the Hudson River Valley, forty miles north of Albany. Every house could be named according to the family who lived there and shared in the community's life.

KNOWING EACH OTHER

Born there, I graduated with basically the same class that started together in kindergarten. The village celebrated holidays with parades, concerts, bazaars, drama and summer festivals. My family of six children and two parents lived in the same home for forty-five years, a home that did not have a lock on any door until 1964. I literally knew everyone in the entire town. My father knew all his customers by their first names and spent time with each one, not only to attend to business but because they were his friends. Everyone mattered. Everyone deserved to be recognized by name. I practiced this behavior naturally in my parish work years later as I would know the names of two thousand adults and children who were a part of the congregation. It was not a technique for satisfying the customer that I learned in seminary. Instead, it was a natural expression of loving the family that came from my experience of a village community.

In 1975 I started a summer camp for youth. Although I passed on the baton of leadership long ago, our family's summer schedule is still arranged around attending the camp because my children cannot even conceive of the possibility of missing this week-long event. What makes this experience so transforming is not the camp's specific activities—though they are planned creatively months in advance—nor is it the beauty of the setting or even the wonderful counselors. Instead, it is the reality that 125 people will live together for seven days, wholly known and wholly loved. The experience of community is so powerful that it has always been necessary to prepare the participants for returning into the "real" and very divided and individualistic society, one that distrusts and isolates its members.

THE COMMUNITY OF WORK

In the team development seminars conducted at the Patnaude Group, participants undergo similar transformations. Even with disparate project teams thrown together with only one common purpose—to meet a deadline on a corporate project—we come to appreciate each other's differences and develop community. These participants also develop such a deep appreciation and trust of each other that they, too, must be prepared for reentering the work world. Back at the office, their new awareness and behavior is often the first thing colleagues notice. If an observer muses, "What happened to him?" we encourage the seminar participants to simply smile and respond, "A lot!"

CHARACTERISTICS OF COMMUNITY

Some aspects of community require hard work and others stem naturally from that effort. The foundation of any of these is trust, the practice discussed fully in Chapter Ten. The following are three aspects of the community experience that I believe are essential.

Communication

Originating from the same root word as community, this skill is the most important one you can develop. In any process of team development, communication must be open, honest, direct, and skillful if the team is to form deep relationships and move to a high performance level. "Open" indicates all information is available; "honest" means all the information is true; "direct" communication is exchanged between the appropriate parties, and "skillful" involves the use of tact and integrity.

Attentiveness

People who share work lives must be attentive to issues that could become obstacles between them. Behavior, motives, and attitudes require periodic evaluation. Staff meetings that evaluate behavior according to established guidelines for community life will achieve far more than those that review just the items on the agenda. Paying attention to "how people are being," as well as what people are "doing," will have a long-term payback.

Celebration

In a true community, people don't simply tolerate those who are different. Rather, knowing that combined differences contri-

bute to strength, they celebrate diversity. True community is a
setting that allows everyone to serve as a leader in some capacity; natural leaders step back while those who are often reserved come forward. All contribute part of their interior
wealth to the beauty of shared leadership.

Community is also a place that allows for adversity; an
arena where people can disagree with integrity, where people
listen, accept differences, and attempt to understand each
other's wounds. If someone needs to stand outside the lines of
community, the community honors the distance yet ultimately
redefines the lines to draw the outsider back in. Edwin
Markham suggests this communal guideline in his poem
"Outwitted":

> He drew a circle that left me out,
> Heretic, rebel, a thing to flout.
> But love and I had the wit to win,
> We drew a circle that took him in.

The celebration of life passages is another aspect of community. Births, deaths, successes, failures, weddings, and di-
vorces are all as much a part of the life of community as they
are of the life of any family. Creating ritual around those events
is a way to not only acknowledge but honor these life passages.

Joy is one of life's greatest gifts and results from genuine
community. Joy comes to us as a product of process. It is something we will discover along the way of a life fully expressed.
As M. Scott Peck writes: "Simply seek happiness, and you are
not likely to find it. Seek to create and love without regard to
your happiness, and you will likely be happy much of the time.
Seeking joy in and of itself will not bring it to you. Do the work
of creating community, and you will obtain it—although never
exactly according to your schedule."

Celebration in Business

In order to lead joyful lives through our work, we must become connected to festive passion, conscious that we are creating productive change, and aware that there are many ways to do the same thing. Elements of light-hearted, intentional celebration include playing without a purpose, calling up humor from the heart; seeking spontaneity and creativity at every possible juncture. Discovering the potential for joy requires an intention for celebration, making time and space for festivity.

We can do so by public recognition of achievements and spontaneous celebrations of our purpose. Celebrations promote teamwork and make work fun, so that we work harder, smarter, and longer. But that is not the primary point—the Art of Intentional Celebration is not a new leadership technique for getting more productivity out of the employed. Its purpose is to encourage the sheer joy of working at our art; the primary criterion for determining a true leader should be a person's ability to create an environment in which it's a pleasure to work. Leaders must lead the way and participate fully. If times are hard, don't stop the festivities, but look for small successes and celebrate those. Create the design for a celebration, involve others in the plan, and implement from the heart. Dare to have fun and listen for the laughter of a spirit at play.

RITUALS

Intentional celebration involves ritual, a channel by which we can establish relation to time, history, and eternity. At work, traditional ribbon-cutting and vessel christening ceremonies are rituals designed to celebrate beginnings and new creations. Similar ceremonies can celebrate newly hired employees. If companies would ritualize the process of introducing new employees into the community at work as we ritualize the process of new membership into spiritual communities or the freshman class at college, the new members would feel as if their feet are on the ground and their presence makes a difference right from the beginning. I know of too many examples in which, after the relationship has been consummated, the new member is left alone in a barren cubicle, with no communication and no community. The new employee feels isolated and unimportant. The practical benefit of low turnover is obvious, but the impact of a meaningful incorporation ritual is a reflection of what the organization believes about the value of its single, most important resource: people.

The rituals of community are perhaps the most historic because our tribal beginnings were based on ritual. Eating together, baptisms, rites of passage, weddings, funerals, physical touching, gifting, singing, and the telling of stories are some of the ways in which communities share their common story and express their love for one another. All of these are applicable, in some way, to the creative and courageous leader whose intention is to create workplaces that help shape the lives of the people who are there to practice their art.

SYMBOLS

Symbols can extend a ritual beyond the event itself. At work, an organization's colors, logo, or flag all serve as symbols that reflect a culture. Gestures ranging from delivery of fresh flowers every month to a week with no other responsibility than visiting as many areas and employees of a corporation as possible can be invaluable in symbolizing appreciation of newly hired employees—or valuable long-time workers. One Chicago-based corporation has found a particularly creative way to provide a symbol of the former radiance of employees who have died: They go to Ingleside's Illinois Star Registry, a private company that actually allows people to purchase unnamed stars, and name a star in honor of their co-worker. Such an action helps colleagues process grief in a positive way, and lets them know that they, too, will be remembered for years of important service.

A Symbol of Light

We encourage the lighting of a special candle whenever someone comes into your office to speak with you about an issue of considerable significance. The ritual of the lighting and the symbol of the light silently indicates your attentiveness. One of our clients who used this approach regularly came back from a break only to discover that the candle was lighted in his absence. Next to the light was a note from a colleague who had previously been suspicious of the candle ritual that read: "I need to talk with you as soon as possible. Please call me."

A Symbol of Permanence

Many organizations overlook one of the most important symbols of the company: the buildings in which it functions. One of the most noble of art forms, architecture provides a symbol for many generations, reflecting the values of the society that built it. Corporations that fail to pay attention to natural light, open space, greenery, sound, color, and art are missing a powerful tool in valuing their employees.

Symbols can be powerful reminders for remembering what we have accomplished in the pursuit of our life purpose and in the celebration of one of life's greatest gifts, joy.

THE JOURNEY OUTWARD

A Way of Action

PURPOSE:

To emerge from the center
intent on serving the vision,
trusting others to assist in a work
that will make a positive difference.

DISCIPLINE FOR MASTERY:

Intention

**PRACTICES OF
INNER MANAGEMENT:**

• Power • Trust
• Compassion

We've explored a way of knowing derived from imagination, intuition, and joy. Now, as we make our way back out of the maze, we consolidate a way of action based on acknowledging power, cultivating trust, and expressing compassion.

If intuition is the process that gives us access to the power of imagination, trust is the key to a more enlightened relationship to power itself and to building an alternative to tyrannical hierarchy. Team development requires trust as its foundation. First, however, we have to learn to trust ourselves.

The EAGLES seminar attracts strong-willed, highly competent individuals who have achieved success by striving and winning in a competitive environment. One might say they epitomize the values of our culture. Because their vigorous individualism will almost certainly emerge in the course of the EAGLES seminar, it is important on that first night to find a means to assure everyone that there can also be common agreement about the structure, purpose, responsibilities, and objectives for the coming year. After a year's conversation, people may become intimate companions or just a familiar company of strangers. It depends upon the degree of commitment to honest communication, confidentiality, preparation, and mutual support. These lay the foundation for an environment of trust generating its own power—power that each can own and share. It means also that everyone will celebrate and suffer the ups and downs of this exploration of leadership together. This is the root meaning of compassion, the culminating practice of inner management.

Within the practice of compassion lies the discovery of a style that enables one to live in harmony not only within the workplace or community, but to affirm a fundamental relationship to the greater universe. Quantum physics has made us aware that at a molecular level we are formed in the same way as everything else in creation. This means that we are sister and brother to each of the hundred billion stars in a hundred billion galaxies and to everything that orbits around them. If love is a legitimate name for the energy that creates and runs the universe, then our capacity to love measures the depth of our connection with the cosmos.

There are signs that signal the presence of love. One of the clearest is compassion. Compassion is the measure of our desire to extend ourselves to others by offering to share both their pain and their joy. Compassion clears the sight for the perception of universal value. When leaders exemplify compassion, their actions serve as symbols for what is right and good. Corporations that are conceived and nurtured by compassionate leadership can play a significant role in shaping the mores of society by basing every action on the dynamic triad of authentic power, willing trust, and a compassionate sense of community.

We may resist the threefold challenge of the journey, much like young eagles reluctant to be pushed from the nest. Yet at the journey's end is the ultimate reward—limitless flight.

7 POWER

The world would have you agree
with its dismal dream of limitations,
but the light would have you soar
like the eagle of your sacred vision.

ALAN COHEN

A CLAMOR LIKE ROLLING THUNDER, columns of green smoke shooting up from the floor. A terrifying portrait projected upon the screen of smoke. From it, a stern and menacing voice rumbles: "I am Oz, the great and powerful...!"

How many children trembled along with Dorothy and her companions as they stood in the great hall in Emerald City, faced with the Wizard's sound and light show? What a relief to discover that it only consisted of smoke and mirrors, that a traveling snake-oil salesman stranded in Oz had jerry-rigged an entire persona. He had fooled everyone until Dorothy looked behind the curtain where, for years, he had been hiding. Unmasked, he was revealed as a mild, somewhat ineffectual little man who had manufactured a show of power to hide his fear of inadequacy.

How often have we witnessed this story re-enacted in the management realm? Leaders manage to hide behind a bravado that masks their insecurities in an attempt to proclaim, "I'm the toughest kid on the block." The dragons of fear, narcissism, and poor self-concept converge, played out as abusive power.

I referred to a certain CEO in Chapter Two who was still trying to prove to his dead father that he was a valuable human being. His leadership style was coercive as he dictated how things would be done, leaving little or no room for discussion. In the leadership role of a hospital emergency room, this approach is valuable and usually required for saving lives. In a corporation or institution, it creates resentment and drains the life out of creativity.

The dragon of narcissism was alive and well in another leader, the head of a small biotech firm in Northern California. Convinced that only his own ideas were worthwhile, he expected immediate compliance and obedience to his demands. In short order, important employees began to jump ship, unable to endure the restrictive atmosphere. Still, the CEO was unwilling to see himself as a part of the problem. When a key senior vice-president threatened to quit, the CEO vowed to do everything possible to prevent this man from ever working in the biotech field if he left. Frightened by this threat, the vice-president acquiesced, and quietly returned to his job. Six months later he quit, claiming that unemployment insurance was preferable to trying to "work in a straitjacket." Others followed suit.

Such examples of the misuse of control and authority are common, and they exemplify a misdirected notion of power. But the behavioral model of commanding and controlling has been passed down through the centuries and serves as a foundation of the old power paradigm. When a feeling of inadequacy reigns, leaders obsessively attempt to control others in the hope of controlling their own overwhelming needs.

What's in It for Me? What's in It for You?

The false and transitory nature of power is a central theme in many of our cherished films, poems, and literary works: A shepherd boy with a slingshot and one well-aimed stone kills a giant armed to the teeth. When David slays Goliath, somehow, we get the feeling that these events transpired as they should—brute power can be toppled by a rock hurled by the frail arm of a boy. In a similar vein, Arthurian legend depicts the Holy Grail being found and won not by the brawny, athletic Lancelot but by the gentle, innocent Sir Parsifal. In assigned readings, students of literature often prowl the ruins of the city of Ozymandias, built by a mythical monarch as a monument to himself, certain it would last forever. Now, however, it lies in ruins. As the poet Shelley wrote, an ironic inscription remains on one shattered stone, an invitation from Ozymandias himself to "look on my works, ye mighty, and despair."

We often describe goodness as a force, but darkness or evil as a power. We also tend to associate power with dominance, control, aggression, mastery over someone else's will. Our fascination with grisly details about the downfall of a famous corporate CEO, or the triumph of a Lee Iacocca against the forces of the Ford Motor Corporation, are clear signs of our contempt for the kind of power generated by top-down management. Although we realize instinctively that it might be prudent to respect brute power, we feel vindicated when those who wield it come to a bad end. Any corporation has the opportunity to become a "power and light" company—where empowerment is preferable to the naked exercise of authority and where service is as much an objective as market dominance.

Authentic Power: A Lesson in Manners

Power that manipulates others for personal or material gain is ego power and differs from the authentic power residing deep within every individual. Authentic power calls for a kind of leadership that produces lasting results. One of my favorite stories illustrating this kind of power comes from Terry Dobson, author of *Safe and Sound: How Not to Be a Victim*. In it, he describes his own need to exhibit external power when ultimately what was required was a power that came from within.

The holder of a black belt in aikido, Terry had always hoped for a legitimate opportunity to use his hard-won craft for rescuing the innocent from the malevolent. Though his master instructor had clearly taught that aikido was an art of reconciliation and peace, Terry's impulses tended toward resolving conflict through force. An incident in a Tokyo train provided him with that opportunity.

As the car doors opened at a transfer station, a large drunk man, filthy and vomit-stained, stumbled aboard the train. Screaming obscenities, he threw a punch at the first person he saw—a woman cradling an infant—which sent her flying into the lap of an elderly couple. The passengers, terrified by the man's rage, huddled into the corners of the train car. Terry stood to confront him. "This is it," he thought. "This is my opportunity to make the world a safe place for decent human beings." The wild, drunken man had another perspective.

"So," he roared. "A foreigner who needs a lesson in manners." The challenge made, the two men squared off to battle, when from the rear of the car came an ear-splitting "Hey!" The intoxicated man reeled around to level the interloper only to behold a tiny, elderly man dressed in a beautiful kimono. In a strangely joyful, lilting tone, the old man spoke: "Come here. Come here and talk with me."

As if on a string, the drunkard was pulled forward until he stood in front of the tiny gentleman. "Talk to you!" bellowed the drunken man. "Why should I talk to you?" Unruffled and without a trace of resentment, the old man asked, "What have you been drinking?" "*I've been drinking sake and it's none of your damn business!*" screamed the man, spattering the older man with flecks of spittle.

"Oh, that's wonderful," the old man said with evident delight. "You see, I love sake too. When I was a younger man, every evening my wife and I would take a little bottle into the garden and sit on the wooden bench that my grandfather's first student made for him. We would watch the sun go down and we would notice the persimmon tree growing. My great-grandfather planted that tree," he continued, all the while looking into the eyes of the large man whose face now was very soft. "Persimmons do not do well after ice storms yet ours has done well, even with poor soil. I just love persimmons."

"Yeah," said the large man, "I love persimmons too," his voice trailing off.

"Yes," said the old gentleman, "and I'm sure you have a wonderful wife, too."

"No," replied the man. "My wife died." He hung his head. Very gently, swaying with the motion of the train, the big man began to sob. "I have no wife, no home. I have no job and no money. I don't know where to go. I am so ashamed of myself." Tears rolled down his cheeks, and a spasm of pure despair rippled through his body.

All this occurred with Terry still standing in his attack position, emanating a "make-the-world-safe" righteousness. Suddenly, Terry felt dirtier than the drunken laborer. It was a lesson in authentic power. As he exited at his train stop, Terry recalls looking back: the large man lay with his head in the older man's lap. Patting his filthy, matted hair, the little man was last heard saying, "There, there. This is very hard. Tell me all about it." As the train pulled away, Terry Dobson sat down on a bench, stunned by the lesson his aikido teacher had tried to impart to him many times in the past: Muscle and meanness are no match for the power of love and a few kind words.

Two Styles of Power

There are two styles of power. Personal power uses pressure and incentive to fulfill clear expectations for others or employs logic and reason to promote one's own point of view. Socialized power uses attraction and bridge building—finding commonalty, calling up a clear vision, disclosing, enrolling, and listening in order to lead others.

Rather than cultivating win/lose situations and feeding off conflict, socialized power seeks win/win outcomes and collaborative solutions. A table of comparison for the two groups, based on Dr. A. Lad Burgin's synopsis and development of McClelland's model, illustrates the contrast:

Socialized Power	Personalized Power
Influencing people	Controlling people
Developing and improving others	Protecting one's own reputation and position
Developing mutually beneficial relationships	Impressing people and gaining status
Including others	Defeating others

Power in Choice

Chapter Two discussed how every turn of the maze confronts us with choices. Access to power offers the same options. We can allow external forces (such as the ego's need for approval or insecurity about resources) to dominate our behavior. To provide quick relief from our fear, we can choose a self-serving, manipulative, and controlling style of power that provides victory through another's loss.

We may also choose the other option, the way of hope, which includes a belief in empowerment. Banking on empowerment means assisting others in discovering their own sources of power and influence. The organizational leader who chooses to coach others to set their own goals, and who gives them responsibility and authority to manage, is the leader who creates a legacy. Rather than controlling, this leader is confirming; instead of overpowering, empowering; rather than pace-setting, participating. In the very act of choosing to follow this path, the leader becomes all the more powerful in the eyes of those who follow.

CHOOSING TO GIVE THAT
WHICH YOU WOULD KEEP

A traditional adage reminds us, "If you truly desire something, give it away and you will have it back tenfold," and I've come to realize that these are wise words to remember. My grandmother kept a book that had been in her family for generations. One of her most prized possessions, it held the key to the story of her family. For some reason, on one of my visits years ago, my grandmother spontaneously handed the chronicle to me and told me it was now mine to keep. Three weeks later, her house burned down, and she lost everything she owned. In a letter to me after the fire, she wrote about how thankful she was that that one cherished heirloom had been saved, and she included this bit of wisdom: "That which I saved, I lost, but that which I gave away, I saved." I have seen the same situation occur with leaders who have learned to give away the power given to them. In the course of giving, their gift significantly increases.

Leaders are consistently challenged by the fact that the power of manipulation and control—something they have ample access to—can be addictive. When we make choices that are healthy for us, deciding not to follow the path of addiction or dysfunction, we gain a level of power a measure above the level of chaos and indecision. Addictions cannot be satisfied; they have unquenchable appetites. Because addictions are founded on the fear of living without a crutch of some sort, addictions can only be transformed by the love that takes their place.

One of my own challenges has been to overcome the need to control, a behavior often motivated by arrogance, an attitude that I "know best." When I am faced with another person who also seeks control, I confront my own dragon. When we choose to empower ourselves each time this challenge surfaces, we diminish the power of the dragon.

In implementing foreign policy, American diplomats have traditionally used a personalized power approach—coercion—as a formula for protecting our global interests. This style of managing conflict has generally meant pressuring the opponent into negotiation. If agreement was not reached, embargoes or military strikes followed. After years of frustrating and humiliating disasters in Vietnam, Cuba, Nicaragua, Angola, and Somalia, it is clear that such use of power is ineffective.

If a new leadership paradigm is to emerge, a more gentle and compassionate diplomacy will as well. The new peacemaker will focus on the problem itself, not on fixing blame. Through creative mediation, negotiators will help channel the passion of violent conflict into constructive, cooperative behavior. The new peacemaker will understand that what is needed is not coercion but communication and compassion. Former president Jimmy Carter is paving the way toward a new style of U.S. diplomacy that examines the causes and effect of international conflicts, proposing creative, nonviolent resolutions. The nonprofit Carter Center in Atlanta, Georgia, focuses on monitoring elections and fostering mediation talks, creating new cultivation techniques for impoverished farmers, and mounting a global attack against several deadly diseases.

The Power of Voice

The human voice has a character all its own—it represents our personal power. How we use this magnificent instrument is an expression of who we are. Courageous speech inspires awe. When a person speaks with conviction, a powerful force envelops the words. We immediately associate King's "I Have a Dream" speech, or Kennedy's proclamation, "Ask not what your country can do for you," with the passion of the heart that proclaimed them. Through those voices, visionary leaders uplifted us and moved us forward.

Discovering voice is the first step in recognizing its power. The voice, for some, has been muted from an early age. "Don't speak unless you're spoken to," "Children should be seen and not heard," "What you say doesn't matter," are blows that can strike us dumb.

Changes Brought About by One Voice

Josetta Walsh, formerly a nun with the Sisters of the Holy Names, is an example of a person who found her voice and said "no" in order to discover a "yes" that awaited her. Josetta Walsh entered the religious order after college and spent most of her life in the service of the Church. Early on, she committed her life to children's education in the footsteps of Maria Montessori, an educator who believed that children could educate themselves by a process of discovery through their senses. Children thrived under her direction, encouraged to pursue discovery through music, movement, and art.

Through their individual processes of discovery, Josetta witnessed what Montessori believed in—the spiritual unfolding of the child: According to Montessori's theory, a child is attracted to an object and moves into a state of deep concentration and observation. Here the child's natural tendency is to "devour" the subject, becoming completely immersed in it, which in turn activates spiritual life within the child. From there, creativity flows. (Such an unfolding is the process of the maze that adults must relearn, yet it is practiced by children instinctively.)

Josetta came to believe that this unfolding needed to be encouraged and safeguarded in the home, a process encompassing the whole family. Risking the unknown, she abdicated her religious community life of thirty-eight years to pursue a path that would aid families in the development of their spiritual lives at home.

Her work resulted in the Child and Family Institute in Menlo Park, California, where children can discover their unique academic, artistic, and personal gifts. Although she is now retired, Josetta Walsh's work lives on, assisting people in creating playful and caring environments where family members can learn supporting and loving behaviors.

Power in "Servant Leadership"

In his ground-breaking book *Servant Leadership*, Robert K. Greenleaf, longtime director of management relations for AT&T, explored the paradoxical notion that the key to great leadership lies in accepting the responsibility of servanthood. Basic to this idea is the leader as seeker, a personality who is always searching, listening, alert to the pulse of new and better ideas. It is this prophetic dimension to leadership that keeps the servant/leader from being just another follower.

Greenleaf began writing his book in 1969, at a time when the United States was in great ferment and sorely in need of new models for leadership. "Caring for persons," he wrote, "is the rock upon which a good society is built." He believed that "servant leadership," stressing listening before action, was attuned to the changing social reality and was a prophetic as well as a practical voice. "I am hopeful for these times...they are challenging the pervasive injustice with more force...and the performance of a whole range of institutions that exist to serve society. A fresh, critical look is being taken at issues of power and authority. People are beginning to learn to relate to one another in less coercive and more creatively supporting ways... [As a consequence] businesses are more questioning of their own adequacy, are more open to innovation, and they are more disposed to take greater risks to find a better way."

In Greenleaf's view, the most fundamental of these risks was for business to become a serving institution, serving not only those who produce but also those who use and consume. He thought of this new ethic in ancient terms—as one step on the Buddhist "eightfold path," namely that of right vocation or livelihood. His concern was that this principle be adopted deeply, rather than applied superficially as an external device to stimulate productivity. Nothing less radical would challenge the venerable leadership tactic of "command and control."

In the twenty-six years since Greenleaf first expressed these thoughts, much of his prophecy has come to pass. The Soviet Union no longer exists as a monolithic political force vying for world domination with capitalist superpowers. The Berlin wall has been demolished, and the division of Germany is now a memory. Even as deadly conflicts over territory and power fragment the peace in the former Yugoslavia, Palestinians and Israelis work toward peace after decades of bitter, rivalrous battle. The nations of Europe stand on the threshold of unprecedented economic cooperation. There is still much progress to be made, but a collaborative spirit is abroad and active on the planet, calling for new ways to exercise power for the common good.

LEADERS AND TRUSTEES

According to Greenleaf's model, given the realities of our times, two kinds of servant/leaders are necessary in every organization: those in active leadership positions, and corporate trustees. An active leadership position may be typified by the executive chairman. Trustees stand outside the organization but share their advice and concerns, overseeing progress.

To become a complete leader requires a compassionate combination of power styles according to Tom Chappell, CEO of Tom's of Maine (which was discussed in Chapter Three). In his 1993 book, *The Soul of a Business: Managing for Profit and the Common Good,* Chappell reminds the developing leader that "you don't have to sell your soul to make your numbers...You can be a hard-driving competitor and still run a business with soul, a business that will always employ the spirits of its people as well as their minds and bodies."

THE MASTER SERVANT

In a World War II military hospital, a nurse was caring for a wounded soldier who had lain on the battlefield for many hours. His exposed muscles had become gangrenous. Concentrating deeply, the nurse painstakingly cleansed the wound. Another soldier walked over to look at the patient and, sickened by the sight of the grotesque wound, said, "I wouldn't do what you're doing for a million dollars." The nurse looked up at him, smiled wisely, and said, "Neither would I."

The great leader is a master servant whose life is a sacramental expression of the values that live within.

The Power of the Feminine

One of the greatest forces moving American business is feminine in character and flows through the heart and spirit of the leader from the inside out. The masculine, in contrast, prefers an external expression of power that has an impact internally only after first being expressed outwardly, an outside-in approach.

In the marketplace, a much needed feminine power is beginning to flower. It will restore balance to what has previously been a masculine domain. The greatest liberation movement that yet remains is the liberation of the woman in every man. That, joined with the emergence of the feminine power of women, will mean the change of the world. The rise in power of the feminine is not a proposal for an Amazon revolution in which men will be subjugated to women. When any dynamic of the human spirit is suppressed under the authority of another dynamic, we take a step backward from wholeness.

The celebration of the feminine is not the province of women alone. Without the great She, we are all impoverished. In the workplace and in other seats of power, women are not yet as present and as powerful as they will eventually be, but in a growing number of arenas, the feminine spirit has silently bypassed security to bring balance to institutions bereft of feminine power.

Great samurai warriors learned poetry before they were allowed to pick up a sword. Today, a number of American football players are learning agility through the practice of ballet. Socrates learned about vision by learning about love from a woman, Diotima. She taught him the connection between mind and heart, He and She. The true challenge is the organization's assimilation of the feminine spirit that resides within each of us.

Personally, I embrace the "She" within me—in fact I often like her better than the He. She reminds me of compassion and acceptance when He likes to confront and judge. She is the womb of the creative ideas from which He charges forth, often prematurely.

The new eagles of business are the ones who strongly embrace their feminine spirit. They are men who understand and delight in the great She; they are women who have balanced their powerful He. They care more about making a difference than making a profit. They are associated with what they do because what they do is what they love. They design products that are masculine and feminine, playful, intimate and individualized. They encourage self-expression and give others the freedom to pursue ideas of their own. They are leaders whose purpose is to serve, not only the people who come into their realm of influence, but the He and She who form the foundation of the spirit that makes them soar.

A Study in Social Empowerment: Dorothy Garner

Like many urban neighborhoods, those adjoining downtown Detroit lie under siege. Inside the homes and projects that line these urban streets are neighbors who fear venturing outside their own front doors. The streets themselves are controlled by drug dealers—often youths who grew up in the neighborhood and who now make their money selling crack. All power appears to be in their hands—not only in the addictive power of the drug itself, but also in the belief of these young people that they rule the streets and can play on the fears of everyday people.

WEPROS—an acronym for "We the People Reclaiming Our Streets"—is one neighborhood group trying to take back its neighborhood from local drug dealers. Today consisting of several hundred members in a dozen local chapters, the organization began with Dorothy Garner. A corrections officer and grandmother whose gift is empowerment, Garner has been blessed with charisma, courage, and apparently boundless energy. To call her a spark plug for the city of Detroit would not do her justice—she is more accurately a transformer.

Garner's work has been recognized and honored in many forums, from civic organizations to radio and television documentaries. Having heard a program about her on National Public Radio in July of 1993, I arranged to interview Garner at her home in the Pilgrim Village section of Detroit. As we talked, it was clear that I was witnessing an individual embodying the quality of empowerment—true leadership from the inside out. "We've fought everything, " she said. "Drugs, people not caring, the neglect of the city. We've had to work at it, to teach people that it's their responsibility to hold the line and improve their property, because it's theirs."

Dorothy Garner leads through deep vision and example: When her grandson got into a fight at school, she resolved to change a place where fighting was a way of life. "I started mentoring those boys," she said. Eventually she began a basketball team, working the time clock, washing the uniforms, coaching the players. The students knew that she considered them important, and this recognition gave them a sense of power based on self-esteem.

Garner's tactic was to organize the neighborhood through the office of the local churches, and draw public attention to houses where drugs were sold. "The basic thing, "she noted, "was to get out there and walk the streets and let crack dealers know... that we were going to fight back. You've got to get rid of the fear, that has been put into the hearts of the people. Drug traffickers instill fear and they take over the community." Her message reached people in other parts of the city. They joined together, marching in each other's neighborhoods on alternating Friday nights, shouting, "We love our neighborhood. Pack all your crack and don't come back."

Dorothy Garner believes in relationship—even with people who scare ordinary people. At the men's prison where she works as a corrections officer, she is known as strictly honest, and willing to help anyone who resolves to help himself. "It makes no difference who the man is," she says. "I will sit down and talk to him, and I will tell a man the truth... and I speak with confidence and respect. I don't embarrass him, I just tell him how he can do better, if he will apply himself."

The deeply religious Garner counts among her mentors the late James and Grace Boggs, two septuagenarians who joined her in her war on drugs from the onset. Grace Boggs explains:

"People come out on the porches and say, 'Thank you, Jesus.' And we say, 'Come on and join us,' They say, 'Next time, next time.' But sometimes they'll come out on the porch and beat their pots and pans in order to show that they support us. And there's a real spirit of hope."

Dorothy Garner's message about leadership? "Our leaders have separated themselves from the people they serve," she says. "It's like a manager who puts his office on the top floor. The little man can't reach it. Everyone has good ideas but little opportunity to share them or show their abilities. I believe in going with the people, not in front of them, not behind them, but with them. I also believe that if you extend a hand, you'll get a hand in return. But you've got to extend that hand. You have to give something of yourself."

What Dorothy Garner gives to others is a sense of her own power, and what she communicates through respect and relationship is the reality of empowerment. She is a servant who raises up other servants and a leader who looks to animate leadership in the people around her.

8 TRUST

Simply trust.
Do not the petals flutter down,
Just so.

ISSA

AN ANCIENT HASIDIC VERSION of the Israelites epic escape from Egypt maintains that the Red Sea parted only when Moses put his foot into the water. Part of what this story teaches us is that a great leader trusts the process and believes that the goal is already beginning to happen. Trust precedes accomplishment.

If we trust that there is meaning in pain, it can provide us a learning opportunity necessary for our wholeness. When we trust that there is power that awaits our claiming, we are empowered to act, and to serve. In trust we enter into a relationship of co-creation with Divine Intelligence. When we await the gifts of a life fully expressed, they will surround us.

Julian of Norwich, a fourteenth-century contemplative and mystic, lived through some of the most perilous of times. Both the Hundred Years War and the plague of the Black Death ravaged England and created a bleak desert, hopelessly parched from an absence of spirit. In its midst she brought a deep and optimistic faith to those who suffered, writing: "All will be well, and all will be well and every manner of thing will be well." Trust is the most difficult part of the journey as it requires the traveler's willingness to acknowledge a power beyond our own, a wisdom far greater than the limitations of our knowledge. Trust is letting go and believing in the reality that "all will be well."

The Roots of Mistrust

In his fascinating book, *What Is Total Quality Control? The Japanese Way,* Dr. Kaoru Ishikawa contrasts the Western production model with the Japanese model, in which the division of inspection and quality control are independent and given far greater power. "For without the power to observe and inspect," Ishikawa writes, "there can be no quality assurance."

According to Ishikawa, the reason why the United States needs 15 percent of the work force in supervisory positions while only 1 percent of Japanese employees supervise is because Americans believe "the basic teachings of Christianity which appear to say that man is, by nature, evil." But none of us enter this world broken and an heir to sin. We can choose a path of irresponsible action that deviates from our intended wholeness, but the path is not our heritage. As Julian of Norwich wrote: "God never began to love us. We have been known and loved from without beginning."

If there is any basic sin of humankind, it is the sin of separation from the Divine Goodness that created us. The story of the Garden of Eden is a choice to separate from God rather than delight in the presence of God. Gandhi held to the Buddhist view that the only real sin was *attavada,* the sin of separateness, and the one who conquers this sin conquers all others.

The Financial Costs of Mistrust

Regardless of why we mistrust others, we bring the expectations of mistrust to work, because we bring that which we know to our work. If we expect mistrust, lack of honor, and deviance of character, we may not be surprised to have our expectations fulfilled (which is why, ostensibly, so many supervisors exist).

The cost of mistrust in business is enormous. In his 1994 book *The Trust Factor,* John Whitney writes: "Mistrust doubles the cost of doing business. An enterprise that is at war with itself will not have the strength or focus to survive and thrive in today's competitive environment." Internal costs of mistrust include extremely inefficient layers of hierarchy that can require enormous amounts of time and money. A plethora of memos, meetings, measurements, and micro-managing can result from an attitude that people need supervision, that they really cannot do their jobs without the help of an overseeing eye. This perception is based upon a presumed incompetence rather than the reality of a poor match between people and their jobs. If the match is poor, management ends up supervising and inspecting instead of performing the higher art of coaching.

If people are well matched, whether in personal relationships or in a work relationship, we make a major step toward diminishing the notion of an "evil nature" and build support toward a doctrine of "Original Goodness."

How does such a "lofty" discussion relate to contemporary upheavals in the corporate world? The current trend of "downsizing" is sowing new seeds of mistrust in our corporations. If John Whitney is correct about the cost to business due to mistrust, of the two million employees who are the current product of re-engineering, most could have been re-employed with the cost-savings derived from creating trusting organizations.

In spite of the recent trend for the flattening of hierarchical systems, the Western system can still easily have four layers of management with a middle band whose primary purpose is not to coach, but to control.

The cost of mistrust is not only an internal issue. External sources can be even more devastating when customers lose faith. Detroit learned this lesson the hard way. Taking the American public's allegiance for granted and serving them some of the gas-guzzling, inefficient 1970s automobiles drained that empire's finances, as once-devoted national customers switched to purchasing Japanese products. Indeed, foreign competition had produced a reliable product, winning the trust of the consumer.

The Deeper Cost of Mistrust

As a teenager, my cousin David worked an entire summer for his father in a small, family-owned roadside restaurant. Instead of receiving pay for his work, David opted for an old car that his father owned. All season he dreamed of summer's end: he would be sixteen and have his very own car. Three days before his work stint was completed, his father sold the car without apology, saying that he needed some extra cash. It left the young man brokenhearted, disillusioned, and filled with rage. Forty years later, David says that experience marked the disintegration of the father/son relationship. He never trusted his father again. One can hardly imagine the benefit of a few dollars when compared to the expense of losing a son.

Building Personal Trust

Building personal trust means transforming the dragon of fear—a force that creates self-doubt, discourages risk-taking, and incites a fear of failure. What can extinguish the dragon of fear? A climate of trust. When we discover the meaning of "I can, I do, I am," we are on the path to our unlimited potential.

SELF TRUST

True leaders trust themselves. Not needing the approval of others, they follow a vision when the odds for its success appear uncertain. Depending on inner resources, the intuitive leader knows that rough times may ensue, but ultimately "all will be well." Trusting in their ability to make sound decisions based on cognitive data and intuition, committed to balance in the midst of turmoil, willing to discover play in the hard work of creating, and able to use power that serves as a catalyst for enlisting support, these leaders exemplify personal trust. They know themselves internally and can depend upon themselves in times of need.

Years ago I chose the eagle as the model of tomorrow's leader because of the character of this remarkably self-trusting creature: Whereas other birds merely fly, the eagle soars.

Spotted at altitudes exceeding 35,000 feet, it competes with high-tech jet planes for a flight path. The bird's strength allows it to carry three times its own weight in flight. Its sharp vision enables it to swoop down to claim its prey more than a thousand feet below.

The eagle serves as an auspicious mentor to its young, pushing them from the nest, yet falling with them in case they require rescue. Should the eaglet fail to learn flight after the first attempt, the parent places the young bird back into the nest only to push it out again. Balanced on wind currents, the eagle can hover motionless over a nest to feed its young. The eagle, which mates for life, is a creature of commitment. In an imaginative and playful partnership, the birds mate while in a free fall thousands of feet above the earth. A creature of inner knowing, when an eagle senses that its end is near, it fastens its talons to a rock and stares into the sun until death arrives to claim it.

Finally, the eagle is a lover of the wind. Whereas most birds seek shelter from storms, the eagle relishes the storms' power, soaring to ever greater heights in the midst of the chaos. The words for spirit and breath in both Hebrew and Greek are also the words for wind. The eagle depends on spirit and its support when soaring to unlimited heights. When we trust in our own abilities and know that spirit calls us to the same unlimitedness, we take the first step in building a climate of trust within our organization by exhibiting trust in ourselves.

Building Organizational Trust

There is no single formula for building the climate of trust within an organization. The reality is that there are as many ways as there are people. Couples that reconcile or families that reunite all find their own path and work out a resolution according to individual needs. When we approach the organization from the perspective of community, there seem to be some basic elements required. The four items suggested here are components necessary in any human system and are found in a healthy family as well as a healthy organization. Let's look at valuing people, leading by example, communicating well, and cooperating.

VALUING PEOPLE

People come before profit. I agree with Hal Rosenbluth's *The Customer Comes Second;* any organization's most important internal resource is its own people. If we awaken to a fire raging in the living room and have to chose between getting our families to safety or moving our material goods, the choice is clear and instantaneous. If organizations pause in their deliberation over what they value most, the recipient of the choice may walk before the affirmation is made.

After all, the purpose of business is not simply to earn money but to provide the best available products and services to customers. If that occurs, money will come. Good companies don't seek sales, they seek to build customer relationships. We at the Patnaude Group offer free training days to the children of our clients every quarter to teach them presentation skills that will enhance their public speaking abilities. Appreciative of having had an opportunity to share our work with their parents, we like to give back some of our time to the leaders of tomorrow. We do this because we enjoy it, but doing it also strengthens our relationship with our clients.

We must move away from Frederick Taylor's belief that workers cannot be trusted and managers are essential for supervising their behavior. When we believe that people are good, competent, and truly want to make a contribution, we do less supervising and more celebrating.

It would be naive to think that there are not some who cheat, lie, and steal—these are programs learned at an early age. A life and attitude of scarcity is a powerful motivation for unlawful behavior. So are unrealistic and over-demanding goals. Like the student who cheats on his prep-school exam in order to please his authoritarian father, the person who lives under the pressure of goals beyond their abilities shrinks rather than expands.

Organizations cannot take on the business of healing all wounds or reprogramming deviant behavior, but they can build trusting environments where people can develop trust and eventually flourish. Environments of trust mean places where employees can fail as well as succeed, where they can be open and honest without fear of retribution, where they can be creative in their risk-taking. Here, recognition has been woven into the fabric of the company. Employees are appreciated for their unique contribution, thanked frequently, and affirmed by the responsibility and authority given to them. Here, people are caught doing things right.

Successful corporations are organizations with strong core values, where people come first. In 1949, when his company, Hewlett-Packard, was barely ten years old, co-founder David Packard spoke before a banquet of the captains of industry. "Management," he said, had "a responsibility to its employees, customers, and the community—not just to the shareholders." The audience looked at him quizzically. Hewlett-Packard has clearly maintained those values for over half a century while simultaneously returning millions of dollars in profits to its shareholders.

One of my associates, Mike Renquist, worked at an oil refining company whose leaders valued possessions over an atmosphere of trust. Although the management and an active public relations department insisted that the company's first priority was to provide an environment of confidence, corporate policy did not coincide with these intentions. In the company cafeteria, stacks of videotapes on worker safety practices sat beside a VCR in Beta rather than the popular VHS format. When Mike asked why the company had chosen the uncommon Beta format, he was told management feared the cassette recorder would be used by employees to view personal videos and that the worker safety tapes would be taken home and not returned. In reality, the safety tapes taken from the company premises for home viewing could be counted on one finger—yet a company was willing to jeopardize the work climate over the cost of a few videotapes.

The Affirmation Chair

We use an exercise in our seminars called the Affirmation Chair, which gives an opportunity to publicly express what co-workers value about each other. A chair is placed in the center of the room, and each member gets the opportunity to sit in the midst of her or his peers. Each person sitting around the chair takes a turn stating the words "What I most value about you is . . ." and then finishes the sentence according to their experience with the seated co-worker. The recipient receives appreciation from each person and is allowed to respond with only two words: "Thank you."

Although most people find that sitting in the chair and receiving the affirmations is more difficult than expressing appreciation to others, all ultimately enjoy and are often moved by hearing what others value in them. I have seen, in action, in countless seminars with every level of corporate employee, what I believe is our most important desire—to be of value, to make a difference. When we experience this, we contribute beyond expectation and move toward our limitless potential.

LEADING BY EXAMPLE

Some years ago, in the high-tech industrial area of California known as Silicon Valley, the IEEE Engineering management society sponsored a president's forum for four consecutive years during which four presidents of Silicon Valley companies were invited to speak to managers. Although leaders such as Andrew Grove and Gene Amdahl often disputed the meaning of leadership, there was one item upon which all sixteen unanimously agreed. The primary characteristic they looked for in hiring any senior manager was integrity. Those chosen had to be individuals of high moral and ethical principles, who backed up their talk with performance.

A primary function of leadership is to set the tone of the environment where people spend much of their adult lives. Management, which in turn creates the dynamics of the work climate by its behavior, takes its cue from those who lead them. When leaders set the standards for integrity, honesty, creativity, and consistency, the organization will reflect that dynamic.

I was recently called in to a county tax assessor's office to develop a one-year strategic operations plan that would revamp the faltering organization. The elected official formerly holding the assessor's position had been jailed for embezzlement.

Though the office had been reassembled under new leadership, the remaining team members were shaken: their former boss's lack of integrity had created a climate of vicious infighting, rumor-mongering, and rampant mistrust.

Data gathered prior to our arrival indicated that strategic planning was hardly the priority. Instead, the employees were obsessed with declarations about who was "dead wood," accusations about who was responsible for failures, and wild rumors about who was sleeping with whom. When my consulting team arrived, we were not surprised to meet a thoroughly disempowered group of ten people in desperate need to learn how to trust one another and put the past behind them. Although the work remains in progress, open, honest, and direct communication has been established and the year-end operation of the office came in under budget. Much of this progress resulted from co-workers coming to trust in each other and in a new process for resolving disputes.

In his book *No Easy Victories*, John Gardner clearly states how a leader's values affect the larger society as well as the people surrounding them:

> Leaders have a significant role in creating the state of mind that is the society. They can serve as symbols of the moral unity of the society. They can express the values that hold the society together. Most important, they can conceive and articulate goals that lift people out of their petty preoccupations, carry them above the conflicts that tear a society apart, and unite them in pursuit of objectives worthy of their best efforts.

There was a time in which our word was all that was required in the honoring of an agreement. For me personally, it still is. I have no contracts with any of my clients because I trust them and they trust me. If I make a time commitment, only a catastrophe could keep me from fulfilling my obligations. The only contract that I have with my associates is to meet the requirements of the Internal Revenue Service for clarifying contractor status. I believe in returning every phone call within twelve hours and that a handshake means commitment. Leadership with integrity means one's word is gold.

Voluntary vulnerability, or a willingness to be open, is a

powerfully attractive characteristic in a leader. Colleagues and co-workers are drawn to openness because it makes them feel like more substantive people. They have gained the leader's trust and now must work to keep it—a safe and satisfying covenant between a leader and those the leader serves. This means being intentionally candid, unguarded, vulnerable to the truth. To be open also means being willing to share the more personal aspects of our lives (realizing that these, too, must be subject to a process of inner ripening before such sharing). Nothing is more intrusive than unprocessed pain masquerading as wisdom.

When a leader is both discerning and open, everyone else feels permission to be so, and the atmosphere becomes both more candid and relaxed. The group can address real issues rather than their cover. When voices discover their power, the experience can be breathtaking. Instead of a polite "No. I don't think that's a very good idea," a person may say, "To tell you the truth, I don't respect the intent of the leadership or the process that is developing."

In leadership, trust results from power that prizes performance, relies on cooperation and communication, maintains a steady flow of information, and shows a commitment to vision and the hard work to achieve it. God has given us two ears and one mouth for a good reason. A leader must model attentive listening. This is a natural product of belief in the value of others and their ability to benefit the whole. Being truly present sharpens the quality of communication. Attentive listening is more than a technique—it is an expression of trust in the value, identity, and ideas of every member of the group. Key phrases for a leader who is not only truly interested in a person's ideas and concerns, but is also prepared to listen:

◎ "Tell me more."
◎ "What are your ideas?"
◎ "How would you handle this?"

The brain can comprehend over a thousand words per minute, whereas speech stumbles along at an average rate of 150 words per minute. Thus, it is not surprising that when we listen, it is a natural temptation for the mind to wander. These basic listening techniques can help the leader to resist this tendency:

- Face the speaker squarely—meet their eyes.
- Pause before replying. (This way, you will not interrupt if the speaker is merely taking a breath—which not only conveys that we are listening, but also allows us additional time to register the point in our mind.)
- Ask questions, both to clarify and to assure the speaker that he or she is being heard.

The leader who encourages an open atmosphere for ideas will encourage the artist within all. When people feel unsafe, they retreat behind protective walls and begin the process of survival. In an atmosphere where all ideas have value, risk-taking is encouraged, and public ridicule is disdained, the doors to creative potential open.

Trust is an honorific in the best sense of the word—it is not conferred suddenly, but earned over time. In the *Harvard Business Review,* Lieutenant General William Pagonis illustrates this point in reflections on the Vietnam war. During the Tet offensive, Pagonis was leading a convoy of six boats along the Mekong Delta on a mission. Having unloaded his troops, he learned that a stranded barge had been trapped upriver, and had come under fire. Conveniently experiencing "radio trouble"—which allowed him to preclude his commander's orders to steer clear of the area—Pagonis asked for volunteers to go back. All the soldiers under his command volunteered. They raced upriver, tracers whizzing overhead, to snap the barge's pilot out of a state of frozen panic, and lead the boat to safety. Years later Pagonis wrote, "One leader's orders had been ignored, and another's followed. Why? Adrenaline was one contributing factor. So was loyalty. But most important was my soldiers' trust in my judgment. Had I not already earned that trust . . . in a thousand undramatic settings, those soldiers would not have followed my lead."

Trust-building, then, is like a sword that is forged over time, in a secure environment, so that it can be unsheathed in a time of crisis. Sometimes that initial environment has been so damaged that it must bse re-created by a third party. Trust is a function of organizational vigor. If an organization is fragile, it requires someone to heal and correct its frailties at the foundation—an architect, a physician, a mentor, or a counselor. Re-creating an organization where trust can grow and thrive is one of the greatest challenges for leadership.

COMMUNICATING EFFECTIVELY AND HONESTLY

The ability of the leader to communicate effectively sets the tone of the organization's communication. When organizations are small, communication can be more immediate. Radian's Don Carlton remembers standing outside the door of his first office and merely raising his voice so the entire company could hear him. "That," he said, "was perfect communication." However, an increase in the size and complexity of an organization can make communication more difficult.

Leaders must be accessible. Leaders physically removed from their employees set up barriers that may not be intentional. "Walking the floor" is a great way to open the door to enhanced relationships and spontaneous communication. Announcing certain days of each week when your office door is open with no appointment necessary can reduce appointment calendars and improve your accessibility. Designating certain hours of the week for phone calls, in which you will actually pick up the phone, removes the sentinel voice mail and produces a more honest and satisfying communication experience.

The availability of information defines the difference between climates of trust and mistrust. When an organization has an abundance of secrets or information that is not readily available, a fragmentation occurs and the organization becomes less whole. Again, Radian Corporation stands as a model: At Radian, no information is unavailable to anyone in the corporation at any time, with the exception of data regarding acquisitions. That information is only confidential until the acquisition is complete, and then, as with everything else, any question will be answered. As Don Carlton said, "If anyone wants to find out the amount of my salary, all they have to do is ask. There is no private information at Radian."

Communicating directly and skillfully primarily requires

common sense. When we talk to other people about a co-worker because of our unwillingness to confront the co-worker directly, it is both unfair to that person and to the others who get drawn into the process. Going to the source is a sensible guideline and the path of a courageous leader. Direct communication also means saying what you mean. If sarcasm, humor, or pretense becomes the vehicle of communication, only the skilled recipient can decipher the meaning behind the message—and the side effect may be that that person will dislike you.

Skillful communication means using good timing, attentive body language, and positive language. Blurting out negative comments in a judgmental voice is not skillful. Anyone can do that. More is expected of a leader. The simple formula of "plus-minus-plus"—sandwiching negative feedback between two positive comments—is a good way to begin and end any feedback session. Focus on the behavior that needs to be corrected, rather than criticizing the person. This is an example of positive feedback:

Gary, the way you have coached Bill is a perfect example of just how good a manager you are. You've been patient and clear in your recommendations. May I make a suggestion to you about the way you work with Alice? You speak to her with a very critical voice, almost as if you see yourself as a parent. Is there some behavior of hers that you consider childlike? Perhaps you can listen to the way you use your voice, and apply the same skills you use so well with Bill. You'll have another very productive contributor in Alice. I know you can help Alice be as successful.

In addition to being open, honest, direct, and skillful, effective communication can also be creative. Some Eskimos resolve conflict through poetry. When conflict arises, the two parties are sent off to write their poems and then return to an impartial jury that was assembled during the creative interlude. The poems are read, judged, and the winner is awarded the resolution to the conflict.

COOPERATION BETWEEN BODY PARTS

Life, for some, is a process of eluding systems. Mandatory systems such as taxation or schooling become something to beat rather than appreciate. Dysfunctional systems, ranging from classrooms to corporate cultures, that use fear to manipulate members for the purpose of achieving goals are abusive or oppressive to the human spirit, and should rightfully be avoided if they cannot be transformed, for they lead to spiritual death.

Other systems, however, are essential as they are created with reason, order, balance, and harmony, a whole comprised of essential parts. The old story of the body parts arguing over which organ is most important is an apt metaphor. As the brain arrogantly comes to assume its primacy, all the heart needs to do is skip several beats to humble the brain.

The need for cooperation may seem too obvious to mention, but it is surprisingly easy to overlook. Business is also a system in which all elements must work together: here, too, the whole is greater than the sum of its parts. Manufacturing is not independent of sales, sales is not independent of research and development. If departments work in a climate of mistrust, they tend to become provincial as they put their own interests above that of other divisions and ultimately above that of the whole corporation.

On one occasion, I was asked to consult between two corporate divisions who were locked in a battle of mistrust, each feeling besieged by the other. The corporation manufactured quality medical equipment. They had a superior product, but the bitter relations between their sales and service departments were causing their national reputation to suffer, and it hamstrung their energy for both marketing and service. 'If we could only stop fighting," one salesperson told me, "we could be number one in the industry." The solution was to help them articulate a common purpose for the company as a whole and to discover how each department works interdependently to achieve that purpose. The two departments worked together far more effectively upon recognizing each other's value.

Cooperation Requires Trust

Trust is at the heart of the cooperative and interdependent relationship of teams. Trust in a team operation requires the use of we, not me. Teams that work interdependently and trust each other become high-performing organizations. More open about feelings, they communicate honestly and directly for greater clarity. If they encounter roadblocks, they can search for alternatives without egos getting in the way. They are highly motivated as they share in influence and outcomes. They achieve great satisfaction in their work and enjoy the closeness of being in a working community with each other.

Flying in a V Formation

High-performing teams achieve their goals faster because there is a common thrust in the same direction. Tasks can be shared and the burden does not have to fall upon the project leader. Whenever any individual is in need of assistance, another team member can offer temporary assistance; if a member has more serious issues, the team members can rally to support her or him. Healthy teams celebrate their diversity and their accomplishments. When they incorporate ritual and symbol into their lives as a joyful expression of celebrating their work as their art, they share an experience similar to any loving family or tribe.

Nature shows us this process at work in the flight of wild geese. As each bird flaps its wings, it creates lift for the subsequent bird. By flying in a "V" formation, the whole flock adds 71 percent greater flying range than if the bird flew alone. Whenever a goose leaves the formation, it suddenly feels the drag and resistance of attempting to fly on its own (and the geese in the formation must work harder to fill its gap).

An equally powerful and poignant example of the absence of internal competition and the support of a team member occurred at the Special Olympics several years ago. As ten youths made their way to the starting line for the 100-meter race, they were filled with excitement. Greeting and embracing each other—unlike most racing participants—these athletes welcomed the challenge of running as fast as possible toward the goal of the finish line. "On your marks, get set ..." and they were off and running with great joy, every step an achievement. Suddenly, halfway down the racing path, a boy in the center of the group tripped, and his body went flying onto the hard, rubberized surface. All other nine participants turned to look, stunned, as their friend lay on the track, knee bleeding.

Collectively, without discussion, they stopped and returned to help their fallen partner. They picked him up, gave him a hug for comfort, and when all were once again set, now at about the fifty-meter line, they ran again, racing together toward the finish line. Now that is teamwork.

Trust and Betrayal

Some people have been hurt so deeply that their blanket policy is to trust nothing and no one. This fear creates an "island unto itself," disconnected and separate from all else. If we allow our experiences of mistrust to become the foundation for our perception, then we will delay the ultimate encounter we will have with trust at the end of our life journey. When we breathe our last breath, we have no choice but to let go. It is then that we will know how life could have been if we had been willing to embrace trust.

The labyrinth is a path that requires trust and commitment. When we are on the path that wends its way toward Center with Dragons lurking in the shadows, we have to trust the process and the knowledge that others have walked this way before us and that we are on the right path. When we arrive at Center we discover a presence of the divine, a sacred intuition that reveals a truth not easily uncovered and often not easily accepted. Trusting in that wisdom is one of our most difficult challenges. When we walk out, ready to take action, we must trust that we are doing what is right and most beneficial. If we do not trust because what we fear is betrayal, then we will never know trust. Betrayal can be as much a part of trust as doubt is a part of believing. It's learning to observe this and move forward mindfully that is the challenge.

9 COMPASSION

Do not weep; do not wax indignant.
Understand.

BARUCH SPINOZA

WHEN WE BEGAN THIS JOURNEY many chapters ago, I said
that one of humankind's greatest fears is the fear of intimacy.
Although each of us ultimately desires to be wholly known and
loved, we often thwart that which we seek. The irony about
seeking intimacy is that the potential for intimacy is all around
us. Indeed, searching for intimacy is like standing waist-high
in a pond, waiting for rain so that we can get wet.

Intimacy envelops us in the interconnectedness of everything in our universe. Compassion comes with acknowledging
that interconnectedness. As Thomas Merton wrote: "The whole
idea of compassion is based on a keen awareness of the inter-
dependence of all these living beings, which are all part of one
another and all involved in one another."

The mystic has always seen all things as interdependent:
no thing is done without effect, no act performed without consequence. The separation between objects may appear to be
real, yet separation and dualism are contrary to the practice of
compassion. When we view our lives as separate, we create a
world of "haves" and "have nots." In such a context any ex-

pression of concern is not compassion, but pity. And pity, as kindly as it may seem, only creates a gulf between the receiver and the giver. Compassion, on the other hand, builds a bridge that makes the giver and receiver one.

The Physics of Compassion

Proponents of chaos theory, such as MIT meteorologist Edward Lorenz, remind us of this principle, reporting that if a moth flaps its wings in tropical Venezuela, a small shift in wind will be felt in central Kansas. Other scientists contend that stands of trees are in pheromonic communication with one another, that they can sense the invasion of a predator and transmit the information one to another. Just how deep is the interdependency of the universe? Is it possible that all creation not only celebrates, but also suffers as one?

There is a clue to that mystery in the night sky. When we stand outside on a summer evening and look at all the galaxies, we know that their light has taken thousands of years to cross the vast reaches of space. But the ancient tapestry of the night shows more than the great age of the cosmos. For nature goes to the same source to create a star as it does to create a gnat. A nebula is made of the same stuff as a neuron. Thus, the stars are more than objects to behold—they show us ourselves.

Quantum field theory has taught us that all things are made of atoms. Atoms, in turn, are made of subatomic particles, which, in fact, are not matter, but actually minuscule fluctuations of energy and information in a void that engulfs them like fish in a vast ocean. Indeed, according to mathematical cosmologist Dr. Brian Swimm, the substance for all of the matter of humankind would fit into the amount of space the size of a pea. If the empty space were removed from the matter of the whole earth, the entire planet could be contained in an area the size of Shea Stadium.

Compassion in the Corporate Community

Compassion springs from our inner sense of certainty that all lives are intertwined. It's what allows us to see the face of a starving child in Somalia and, just for a moment, to discern the face of our own child. It allows us to enter and experience the pain and joy in another person's world. No relationship, however committed, intimate, or passionate, will survive for long without compassion.

If the business world took to heart the axiom that all things are connected, corporations would accept the fact that nothing can be added to the environment without having an impact on everything else. All creation is interconnected, as is every person living on the globe. No quest, no enterprise, no company of friends, strangers, or co-workers, can find purpose without the last great gift of compassion, the root of empathy or, as Dostoyevski put it, the intelligence of the heart. The visions that we provide for our organizations are limited only by our ability to keep that fundamental principle in focus.

In *The Soul of a Business,* Tom Chappell writes: "I know that we—the business community—can change our traditional business culture. The mind will calculate forever, but the heart will eventually give in. We need to help each other. Whatever our differences, our strength is in affirming our identity, joining together to solve our common problems and aspiring to our common aims—to rebuild our community life, to clean up our local waters and air, to reach out to our needy neighbors, to reseed the village green."

Starting at the Bottom

Wayne Patrick is President of Erie Industries, a large tool and die shop in Ferndale, Michigan. Though his father founded the business forty-three years ago, Wayne did not succeed to the leadership of this thriving company merely because he was the boss's son. He began to work in the family business after finishing college, not in the office as an aspiring young executive, but on the floor as an entry-level toolmaker. Wayne spent long hours on his feet, learning every aspect of the exacting art of machining tools. He moved through the craftsman's chairs, first serving as an apprentice, then a journeyman. His mentors were those blue-shirted men who had been toolmakers in the business long before Wayne had been born. He received no preferential treatment, no privileged status. In fact, he had to work harder under the scrutiny of his employees-to-be. After ten years on the floor and an additional eight years in management, Wayne did become president of the corporation. But he had earned the accolade by learning his business from the "inside out."

Thomas J. Watson of IBM and Bill Hewlett of Hewlett-Packard are legendary for regularly walking the plant floor to meet employees where they actually worked. They believed that the floor provided the best place from which to manage, as it gave them a vantage point and experience with what was real for a majority of their workers. I see this concept as it relates to the quality of compassion. The word compassion comes from the Latin verb *compati*, which means to suffer with. Compassion requires that we go where it hurts, where there is trouble or pain, and enter fully into the anguish and brokenness that reside there. We cannot stand above or outside the experience but instead must enter into it in order to suffer with the one who suffers. It requires being vulnerable with the vulnerable, powerless with the powerless, and weak with the weak. Compassion is the experience of being fully immersed in the condition of being human. Compassion is the essence of living a life fully expressed.

EXPERIENCING SUFFERING

We can't take away the difficulties people face, but we can choose to share in their suffering, their loss. We often cannot solve the problems of others, but we can make an attempt to hear those problems and to shoulder them along with the person. Sometimes it's the best thing for them, and for us.

I believe that corporate organizations, our business and our work, have such a human purpose. Corporations are on this planet not only to make products and to provide a place for people to work, but also to leave a legacy, a gift that will last for generations to come.

ALLEVIATING SUFFERING

Many suffer within company walls because of the environment that the organization creates. Dependency, loss of positive self-concept, and fear of failure are just some of the factors created by high-stress workplaces. Such places can break the human spirit. For the leader, the first step in healing these destructive ways is to identify with those who are paralyzed and understand their struggle. From that understanding comes more of an awareness as to how those negative conditions can be changed.

Those of us outside the corporate walls suffer, too, because we share the same planet home that is dying from misuse. Many corporations continue to depend upon the resources of this earth to meet their bottom line, quarter after quarter. The creative forces of the human mind and the toil of human hands are joined to raw materials in order to make companies profitable. However, the polluting of the earth has reached staggering and nearly irreversible proportions. Our challenge today is to return the gift back to the forces that have given so readily to make this all possible. The best thing we can do for this planet is to befriend it in its time of need. It's the best act we can do for ourselves as well.

How can companies combine making a profit and having a compassionate purpose? It is essential that companies remain profitable in order to stay in existence. Although concern for the bottom line is essential, it is not the purpose of our work. There is more to life than making money. There is an opportunity to serve.

In interviewing participants of a CEO EAGLES program, I discovered that many executives today are retraining their sight to discern compassionate purpose as well as to look for profit. This shift in consciousness is manifested in small but significant ways. A bank president encouraged employees of his bank to get involved in community organizations and gave them time off from their daily work at the bank to be involved with groups around the city. In another case, the owner of a small and emerging biotechnical firm indicated that they were taking a pro-active stand on regulatory controls—noting that "it doesn't cost more to do it right. It just requires more work." This executive said that one person on his staff spends half of his time on regulations alone. And in the development process for a new solvent, they were committed from the beginning to making it water-based, despite the documentary hassle. It took more time and cost the company additional money, but in the long run it would be far more beneficial to the environment, and that was the priority this founder and his company resolved to heed.

Leading with Compassion

IN BUSINESS

It is often difficult for powerful corporate executives to resist the lure of individual aggrandizement, but it is becoming more clear that the cooperative picture is far more important. This has emerged most forcefully in Detroit, where the CEOs of the automotive industry's Big Three are all very much team players rather than princes of a corporate empire.

Regarding the workplace community, a startling development is the dawning of an era of "no more stars." Twenty years ago I had the opportunity to work with the president of General Motors. Whenever he walked into a room, his presence created a sense of nearly fearful awe. Today, modern company leaders such as Chrysler's Bob Eaton, Ford's Alex Trotman, and GM's Jack Smith are assuming a new, very different posture from their predecessors. According to Time magazine, Detroit's three new CEO's have introduced a similar management style: "Modesty, humor (especially of the self-deflating variety), open discussion, candor, and team play are all in. Pomp, protocol, pretension, and paperwork are distinctly out."

According to traditional workplace roles, entrepreneurial spirit was expected only of senior management. Nowadays, needs have changed, and that trait is encouraged in all levels of the corporation. Our talents can be transformed from tools of competition to assets of community. Interestingly, this is also coming to mean the demise of middle management. As complex organizations flatten out, employees' talents catalyze unification.

Such cooperation gave birth to an organization that improved the quality of microchip manufacturing throughout the nation. Sematech, a consortium of microprocessor companies, and the U.S. government joined forces to research new ways to design and manufacture their product. As a result of

Sematech's success, the American chip industry—having been overshadowed by Japanese manufacturers—has bounced back and now leads the industry.

How can business leaders meet the challenge of serving and leading a society that has been locked into alienation—and the loneliness that results from it—to move toward mutual support and cooperation? The first step perhaps is to recognize our desire for authentic unity, to be "at home" in a real community, not driven or forced together but drawn together through natural ties. We are tribal beings, and the narcissistic and obsessive individualism of the last several decades has been one of the most divisive currents in the history of our century. Perhaps, for a period of time, this stage was essential—as is, say, the adolescent's establishment of the ego. But with the phasing out of corporate "stars," all members of the business community begin to walk the same path. Teamwork creates solidarity, the truest expression of compassion.

Compassion, therefore, is not simply a new skill for leading. Throughout California's Silicon Valley, companies are working cooperatively to be more effective and efficient, even while they remain in competition in the global marketplace. After recognizing our desire for unity and embracing it, we can recognize each other's gifts.

IN MEDICINE

By working together with a common understanding and a common bond, we will successfully conquer the suffering of our world. Some of the most profound examples of such victories can be found in the medical field and in the compassionate professionals who find new ways to honor the body that they serve and heal.

Associations with Stanford Hospital in Palo Alto, California, led me to speak with researchers whose treatment philosophies are a far cry from the brutal paradigm known as "cut, poison, and burn." Their quest is to heal with a minimum of intrusion. One noninvasive method they have developed uses a new device to essentially pass over the skin to analyze blood without blood ever being drawn.

In therapies of the past, all areas around a tumor might be removed along with the malignant growth for lack of an instrument that could isolate the tumor. Now a specialized technique, using radiosurgical instruments created by Dr. John R. Adler, allows cancer therapy radiation to be so specifically targeted that only the cancerous tissue is affected.

The procedure, developed by Adler (and others) at considerable expense—some out of his own pocket—was the result of his desire to have a more effective therapy for the human body. But when I asked him why he did this, his response was, "Because I saw so much destruction in the prior therapies that I was driven to develop something that would be more gentle and more compassionate."

IN GOVERNMENT

The huge drop in crime in a single year experienced by the impoverished community of East Palo Alto, California, is a powerful endorsement of local governments working cooperatively. In 1992, a record forty-two killings earned the city of only 24,000 people a grisly reputation—"Murder Capital of America." Yet in 1993, dramatically, violent deaths dropped 86 percent. How did this happen? Was there some miraculous transformation in the mood or attitude of criminals who once traumatized East Palo Alto? Hardly. What catalyzed the change was an offer of help from the adjoining cities of Palo Alto and Menlo Park, who concluded that the neighboring town's crime crisis was not exclusively "its" problem, but a regional one.

In late 1992, police chiefs from the three cities created a "red team" made up of six officers whose mission was to seek out drug dealers and career criminals. In addition, the county sheriff's office assigned twenty deputies to aid East Palo Alto's thirty-five-member force. Next, the California Highway Patrol hopped aboard, agreeing to contribute round-the-clock patrols. By spring of 1993, all the pieces were in place for a thirty-eight-member multi-jurisdictional force to begin patrolling the city. Because these residents—ordinarily separated from each other by culture and income—realized their connection with one another, children again are playing in the streets of East Palo Alto. Instead of remaining indignant and separated, compassion allowed neighbors to respond with understanding and effective action.

IN SOCIETY

Experience is the best teacher and reflection on experience the bearer of wisdom. Streetwise men and women have this lesson impressed upon them as children. I came to know this later in life, after having served for years as a pastoral counselor to others in times of crisis. Realizing I had never really experienced any significant crisis in my life, I felt a need to invest my life with greater authenticity by seeking wisdom born of personal experience.

This is what led me to spend several days on the streets of San Francisco with homeless people, experiencing their plight. For me, years of working with homeless people while serving in a parish church in Menlo Park, California, had stripped away most of the discomfort that financially secure people initially feel while in the presence of those who haven't a home. Because of this earlier work, it wasn't uncommon for me to give the homeless some cash or make them a lunch, provide them a job or an attentive ear, but I had never really experienced the impact of homelessness firsthand. I felt ill-prepared to comment on the meaning of homelessness for myself, for community, or for society.

To help prepare myself, I decided to become "homeless" for a few days. I made my way to the city with no cash, identification, or credit cards to rescue me in case of a sudden loss of heart. My body was already feeling the pangs of a voluntary two-day fast, which I had undertaken to prepare me for the experience. On the street only a short distance from the city center, I realized I was already cold and hungry, even though my brief sojourn had only begun.

I spent part of my first day in San Francisco helping an army of volunteers feed some two thousand people in one day at Glide Memorial Church, a refuge for citizens of the city's often brutal Tenderloin district. Watching the endless line file past, each person with a tray of savory beef stew and hearty bread, along with salad and dessert, I could hardly restrain my own desires to get in line and began to imagine something of the desperation a person can feel when really in need of a square meal.

After my shift at Glide, I made some unlikely new acquaintances. One in particular, a man named Mitchell, was fifty-seven years old, epileptic, alcoholic, unable to work, and yet actively engaged in his struggle for life. As many people on the street do, Mitchell kept his possessions in a stolen shopping cart. Like a sentry guarding an unfriendly border, he kept watch over his cart zealously; it contained everything he owned. On the street, he said, everything can be taken away in the time it takes to tie your shoes.

Shortly after he arrived in San Francisco from Tacoma, someone had kicked out Mitchell's left eye during a street confrontation. Despite this and a thousand smaller trials, Mitchell remained gentle and peaceful, with a network of allies and friends. Many people stopped to greet him as we sat on the sidewalk, our backs against a solid wall. After some time had passed, a much younger man appeared on the scene. Mitchell informed me that he and his friend took turns sleeping throughout the night, one guarding their things while the other slept. As Mitchell told me, solidarity was essential here.

As an individual, I can do only a little to alleviate the sufferings of the homeless people of San Francisco—of this nation. Homelessness and hunger are extensive problems that will require the creativity of many communities in tandem to find a compassionate and effective solution. But part of what I might do is to share Mitchell's pain. In the midst of an impossible situation, I sense the spirit and power that makes all things possible. By bonding with his community in their struggle, I become part of a closely woven fabric of human lives. This way, when I later contribute to helping to solve homelessness, it will not stem from pity, but from having had a small taste of the struggle.

As individuals, we are overwhelmed by the needs and sufferings of the world. We are bombarded by story after story of suffering and disaster, until we turn a deaf ear. The relentless din of the news may leave us feeling entirely impotent. However, by bonding together, we can make a difference. If we can allow that suffering into our own reflective experience, we can become empowered by forming a community in which there is unlimited space for strangers.

Crawling Beneath the Blankets of Despair

Several years ago, at a nearby hospital an event occurred that celebrates compassion as the way of imparting integrity to the life we share. The nursing staff at this hospital was having difficulty with an aged man's difficult temperament. He refused to allow anyone into his room and was often so negative that staff members could not even administer medication. One day, an insightful nurse decided to ask a friend of hers to make a difference in this man's life.

That evening, while the man lay quietly glowering in his bed, the door slowly opened into his dimly lit room. As his eyes shot toward the doorway, ready to command a dismissal, he was struck by a figure that stood silently staring at him. It was not the usual "intrusive" staff member, but instead, a circus clown. His features shimmering with face paint, the character sprinted to the patient's bedside. "Move over!" he shouted.

Startled by the order, the old man slid aside as the clown climbed into bed with him. Adjusting the blankets, the clown settled in, paging through a book he had brought. "I'm going to read to you," he said, as he began: "Jack and Jill went up the hill to fetch a pail of water. Jack fell down and broke his crown and Jill came tumbling after." The clown continued on through the collection of Mother Goose as the man listened intently, his body calming with each page. By the reading's end, the once sullen old man lay nestled against his playful visitor, feeling a sense of peace no staff member had ever witnessed. The clown, upon leaving, kissed the man on his forehead and said good-bye. That night, the patient quietly and effortlessly moved into the next life, his face displaying contentment and peace.

Bringing Compassion into Corporate Culture

As contemporary leaders, we have many pressing and difficult realities with which to contend: Today, many employees are being forced to exit the corporate community due to "downsizing." As leaders, do we absolve ourselves because they have received a "good package" for severance? Or do we feel the pain of someone who has lost their work—the vehicle for their art?

What is corporate culture? What does it consist of? Corporate culture is composed of passion and purpose, but also of people with pain and human needs. Do we suffer with those who fear success enough to thwart their potential and bury their gifts? Do we ache with those who fear failure enough to lie or boast a false self? As leaders, when we are able to truly identify with those whom we lead, we take the first step toward a wholeness we all seek and from which we all benefit.

Compassion is the culmination of the journey through the maze, the lens that allows us to see clearly as we look back to take stock of where we have been. It is not an achievement but a process, one that provides the "glue" that holds all the practices of inner management in balance.

Emerging

When the traveler emerges from the labyrinth, the real journey has begun. If the labyrinth has worked its power, we, the traveler, emerge less burdened, wiser, and ready to act. Aflame with passion and defined by purpose, our work will become an art form, a gift to others. Connected to all things, our compassion stirs easily, and we are able to crawl out from under the covers of despair.

Questions for the Ongoing Journey

As we travel inward and outward through the maze, we ask ourselves the following questions:

◎ Do we recognize that we are all on a journey and that where we are is exactly where we are supposed to be? Can we be patient with ourselves and with others in remembering that there is more to become?

◎ Can we identify so closely with the consequence of each choice that we will make decisions that result in integrity and truth and contribute to doing what is right?

◎ Out of caring for ourselves, are we willing to let go of the dragons and restore a much desired balance to our frantic lives? Will we be so committed to balance that we will create healthy and whole workplaces, wherein all who pass through will be stronger, healthier, and happier leaving than when they entered?

◎ Are we courageous enough to identify so deeply with the universe's divine imagination that we will access the creativity necessary to provide solutions to questions that seem unanswerable?

◎ Can we be silent long enough to listen to the inner voice of intuition that speaks from the heart to confirm what the mind has pondered?

◎ Can we remain vital, grounded, and grateful enough to celebrate life as joy with all of its pain as well as its delight?

◎ Will we have courage enough to discover the authentic power of serving that brings us to touch the lives of those in need?

◎ In turn, are we courageous enough to trust others to touch our lives as we discover that we are not separate from those in need; we are those in need?

◎ Finally, will we allow compassion to serve as our mentor, our guide to discovering the deepest expression of who we are?

What if, within our organizations, our work became the practice of compassion—the practice of seeing with new eyes for the express purpose of encouraging integrity in ourselves and our co-workers? We might discover a loneliness, a hunger to make a contribution and a difference, and a thirst for spirit in the workplace among those with whom we work—all previously hidden behind pretense or protected by dragons. Time and time again, I have seen that for most authentic leaders, money is not the ultimate goal or value. What they seek is to make a contribution and to see that their work has meaning.

Historically, human beings and their activities have created problems that others—enlightened leaders—have had to solve decades later. Unmitigated fear has incited individuals to turn against other individuals, nation against nation.

The maze is a divine puzzle that holds ancient yet powerful answers to current problems. Until very recently, we have accepted the illusion that we live in an infinitely expanding frontier with limitless natural resources. Consequently, we have even turned against our own natural environment as we reach for domination and control.

When we drop labor that defiles and harms our earth and when we assume the mantle of a leader who feels compassion for all co-workers and fellow planet dwellers, then our work will be our joy. When we transform our work from a duty to our delight, the world around us will change markedly.

The journey in and out of the maze takes leadership to a new level of meaning, a place of authentic solutions. To travel the winding road to the inner self is the most important journey we make. Within the maze, discoveries are made and inspiration received. It is a path we are called to walk, an ancient path, but one that will lead to a momentous new direction for the powerful leaders of today and tomorrow.

Two-thousand-year-old graffiti carved into a painted column in the house of Lucretius in Pompeii. Inscription reads: Labyrinthus, hic habitat minotaurus. *(Labyrinth, home of the Minotaur).*

BIBLIOGRAPHY

Artress, Lauren. *Walking a Sacred Path: Rediscovering the Labyrinth as a Spiritual Tool.* New York: Riverhead Books, 1995.

Bellah, Robert N. *Habits of the Heart: Individualism and Commitment in American Life.* New York: HarperCollins, 1986.

Blake, William. *The Complete Poetry and Prose of William Blake.* Revised ed. Edited by David V. Erdman. Berkeley: University of California Press, 1981.

Briggs, John, and F. David Peat. *Turbulent Mirror: An Illustrated Guide to Chaos Theory and the Science of Wholeness.* New York: Harper and Row, 1989.

Buechner, Frederick. *The Sacred Journey.* First ed. San Francisco: Harper and Row, 1982.

Cameron, Julia. *The Artist's Way: A Spiritual Path to Higher Creativity.* New York: Jeremy P. Tarcher, 1992.

Campbell, Joseph, and Bill Moyers. *The Power of Myth.* New York: Doubleday, 1988.

Chappell, Tom. *The Soul of a Business: Managing for Profit and the Common Goals.* New York: Bantam Books, 1994.

Cox, Harvey. *The Feast of Fools: A Theological Essay on Festivity and Fantasy.* Cambridge, Mass.: Howard University Press, 1969.

de Tocqueville, Alexis. *Democracy in America.* Trans. by George Lawrence, ed. by J. P. Mayer. New York: HarperCollins, 1988.

Douglas-Klotz, Neil. *Prayers of the Cosmos.* San Francisco: Harper, 1993.

Doyle, Brenden. *Meditations with Julian of Norwich.* Santa Fe: Bear and Company, 1986. (Out of print.)

Drucker, Peter F. *The Practice of Management.* New York: Harper Business, 1954, 1993.

————. *Management: Tests, Responsibilities, Practices.* New York: Harper Business, 1973, 1993.

Fox, Matthew. *Illuminations of Hildegard of Bingen.* Santa Fe: Bear and Company, 1985.

Gardner, John W. *No Easy Victories.* New York: Harper and Row, 1968. (Out of print.)

Gibran, Kahlil. *The Prophet.* New York: Knopf, 1995.

Greenleaf, Robert K. *Servant Leadership: A Journey into the Nature of Legitimate Power and Greatness.* New York: Paulist Press, 1977.

Hall, Edward Twitchell. *Beyond Culture.* New York: Doubleday, 1977.

Hoffer, Eric. *The Passionate State of Mind.* Cutchogue, N.Y.: Buccaneer Books, 1993.

Howard, Robert. *Brave New Workplace.* New York: Penguin Books, 1985. (Out of print.)

Johnston, William (ed.). *The Cloud of Unknowing & the Book of Privy Counseling.* New York: Doubleday, 1973.

Julian of Norwich. *Showings.* Trans. by Edmund Colledge and James Walsh. Ramsey, N.J.: Paulist Press, 1978. (Out of print.)

Keats, John. *The Complete Poetical Works.* Boston: Houghton Mifflin, 1899. (Out of print.)

Kobayashi, Issa. *A Few Flies and I, Haiku.* New York: Pantheon Books, 1969. (Out of print.)

Leslie, Stuart W. *Boss Kettering: Wizard of General Motors.* New York: Columbia University Press, 1986.

Lonegren, Sig. *Labyrinths: Ancient Myths and Modern Uses.* Glastonbury, U.K.: Gothic Image Publications, 1991.

Maslow, Abraham H. *Motivation and Personality.* New York: Harper and Brothers, 1954. (Out of print.)

Mayo, Elton. *The Human Problems of an Industrial Civilization.* New York: Macmillan, 1933.

————. *The Social Problems of an Industrial Civilization.* Cambridge, Mass.: Howard University Press, 1945.

McGregor, Douglas. *The Human Side of Enterprise.* New York: McGraw-Hill, 1985.

Merton, Thomas. *Love and Living.* Ed. by Naomi Burton Stone and Patrick Hart. Orlando, Fla.: Harcourt, Brace, and Co., 1985.

————. *The Hidden Ground of Love: The Letters of Thomas Merton on Religious Experience and Social Concerns.* Sel. by William Shannon. Orlando, Fla.: Harcourt, Brace, and Co., 1993.

Nouwen, Henri J. *The Road to Daybreak: A Spiritual Journey.* New York: Doubleday, 1988.

Ornish, Dean. *Dr. Dean Ornish's Program for Reversing Heart Disease.* New York: Random House, 1990.

Parker, Barry R. *Einstein's Dream: The Search for a Unified Theory of the Universe.* New York: Plenum Press, 1986.

Peck, M. Scott. *The Road Less Traveled.* New York: Simon and Schuster, 1985.

——————. *People of the Lie.* New York: Simon and Schuster, 1985.

——————. *The Different Drum: Community Making and Peace.* New York: Simon and Schuster, 1987.

Peters, Thomas J., and Robert H. Waterman, Jr. *In Search of Excellence: Lessons from America's Best-Run Companies.* New York: HarperCollins, 1982.

Rackham, H. *Aristotle: The Nicomachean Ethics.* Cambridge, Mass.: Harvard University Press, 1934. (Out of print.)

Ray, Michael, and Rochelle Myers. *Creativity in Business.* New York: Doubleday, 1989.

Rilke, Rainer Maria. *The Migration of Powers.* Port Townsend, Wash.: Graywolf Press, 1984. (Out of print.)

Rosenbluth, Hal F. *The Customer Comes Second, and Other Secrets of Exceptional Service.* New York: Morrow, 1992

Salk, Jonas. *Anatomy of Reality: Merging of Intuition and Reason.* Newuj York: Columbia University Press, 1983.

Sallis, John and Kenneth Maly (eds.) *Heraclitean Fragments: A companion Volume to the Heidegger/Fink Seminar on Heraclitus.* University of Alabama Press, 1980. (Out of print.)

SARK. *A Creative Companion.* Berkeley, Cal.: Celestial Arts, 1991.

——————. *Inspiration Sandwich* Berkeley, Cal.: Celestial Arts, 1992.

Schumacher, E. F. *Small Is Beautiful: Economics as if People Mattered.* New York: HarperCollins, 1973, 1989.

Sheehy, Gail. *Passages: Predictable Crises of Adult Life.* New York: Bantam, 1984.

Sheldrake, Rupert. *A New Science of Life: The Hypothesis of Morphic Resonance.* Rochester, Vt.: Inner Traditions, 1981, 1995.

——————. *The Presence of the Past: Morphic Resonance and the Habits of Nature.* New York: Random House, 1989.

Jung, Carl G. *The Essential Jung.* Ed. by Anthony Storr. Princeton, N.J.: Princeton University Press, 1983.

Taylor, Frederick. *The Principles of Scientific Management.* New York: Harper and Row, 1911, 1939, and 1947. (Out of print.)

Tzu, Lao. *Tao te Ching.* Trans. by Ch'u Ta-Kao. New York: Routledge, Chapman, and Hall, 1990.

Vaill, Peter B. *Managing as a Performing Art: New Ideas for a World of Chaotic Change.* San Francisco: Jossey-Bass Publishers, 1989.

Ward, Aileen. *The Poems of John Keats.* New York: The Heritage Press, 1966. (Out of print.)

Watts, Alan Wilson. *The Spirit of Zen: A Way of Life, Work, and Art in the Far East.* New York: Grove Atlantic, 1960, 1987.

Whitman, Walt. *The Complete Poetry and Prose of Walt Whitman.* Garden City, N.Y.: Garden City Books, 1948. (Out of print.)

Whitney, John O. *The Trust Factor: Liberating Profits and Restoring Corporate Vitality.* New York: McGraw-Hill, Inc., 1993.

Yutang, Lin. *On the Wisdom of America.* New York: The John Day Company, 1950. (Out of print.)

Zall, Paul M. (ed.) *Mark Twain Laughing: Humorous Anecdotes by and About Samuel L. Clemens.* Knoxville, Tenn.: The University of Tennessee Press, 1985. (Out of print.)

"Walking a Sacred Path: The Poster." Based on Dr. Lauren Artress's book, this poster illustrates the famed Chartres Cathedral labyrinth in rich, muted hues, accompanied by a brief meditation on the meaning of the labyrinth. Available from Celestial Arts, at 800-841-BOOK.